DISCARD

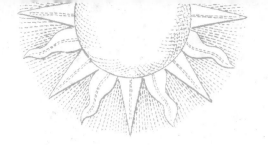

THE GREAT
HISPANIC HERITAGE

Ellen Ochoa

THE GREAT HISPANIC HERITAGE

THE GREAT
HISPANIC HERITAGE

Ellen Ochoa

Judy L. Hasday

CHELSEA HOUSE
PUBLISHERS
An imprint of Infobase Publishing

In memory of Rosanne Deardorff Ochoa—a truly remarkable woman.
Inspiring her five children, Beth, Monte, Ellen, Tyler, and Wilson
to be the best they can be, is a testament to their successes today
and a tribute to her lifelong love of learning.

Ellen Ochoa

Copyright © 2007 by Infobase Publishing

Chelsea House
An imprint of Infobase Publishing
132 West 31st Street
New York NY 10001

Library of Congress Cataloging-in-Publication Data

Hasday, Judy L., 1957-
  Ellen Ochoa / Judy L. Hasday.
    p. cm. — (The great Hispanic heritage)
  Includes bibliographical references and index.
  ISBN 0-7910-8842-1 (hardcover)
  1. Ochoa, Ellen—Juvenile literature. 2. Women astronauts—United States—
Biography—Juvenile literature. 3. Astronauts—United States—Biography—Juvenile
literature. 4. Hispanic American women—Biography—Juvenile literature. I. Title.
  TL789.85.O25H37 2006
  629.450092—dc22   2006019632

Series design by Terry Mallon/Keith Trego
Cover design by Keith Trego

Printed in the United States of America

Bang EJB 10 9 8 7 6 5 4 3 2 1

This book is printed on acid-free paper.

Table of Contents

1

Obviously a Major Malfunction

"To understand and protect our home planet; to explore the Universe and search for life; to inspire the next generation of explorers . . . as only NASA can."[1] These words define the mission of the National Aeronautics and Space Administration (NASA). Incorporated into its *STS-107 Columbia* mission overview memo, this simple yet ambitious statement reminded the press and the public of NASA's purpose in continuing its human space flight missions.

The prime objective of *STS-107*, NASA's one hundred thirteenth space shuttle mission, was to expand on research studies that might provide information to help improve life on Earth. The Columbia crew of seven astronauts included a special member of the team—Ilan Ramon, the first astronaut from the country of Israel. The crew was supposed to spend 16 days in space, working 24 hours a day in two alternating shifts, to conduct more than 80 experiments.

Although the launch of mission *STS-107* seemed to go perfectly, a minor accident at liftoff would lead to disaster when the spacecraft was returning to Earth. Pictured here is the space shuttle *Columbia* shortly after liftoff on January 16, 2003.

A NEW POSITION

All shuttle missions are exciting and create a heightened level of interest in the NASA organization. *STS-107* was no exception. This mission had some unique aspects. Not only was the work aboard the shuttle going to be taking place 24 hours a day, with an international astronaut joining the American crew, but it was also going to be NASA astronaut Ellen Ochoa's first mission in her new post as deputy director of the Flight Crew Operations Directorate. A veteran of four shuttle flights, including two trips to the International Space Station (ISS), Ochoa was now going to experience space flight from the other side, observing *STS-107*'s launch from a seat inside the Launch Control Center. As part of the Mission Management Team (MMT), Ochoa was only in her sixteenth day in her new position on the day of the launch, and had flown out from Houston, Texas, to take part in the management oversight of the liftoff.

A SPECIAL BREED

The seven astronauts assigned to the *STS-107* mission included Commander Rick Husband, Pilot William McCool, Fight Engineer Kalpana Chawla, Payload Commander Michael Anderson, Payload Specialist Ilan Ramon, and mission specialists Laurel Clark and David Brown. Four of the seven astronauts—McCool, Brown, Clark, and Ramon—would be making their first voyage into space. All of them were aware of the dangers of space flight. This crew was particularly conscious of the perils that could befall an astronaut. *STS-107* was the eighty-eighth mission launched after the space shuttle *Challenger* exploded 73 seconds after takeoff from Florida's Kennedy Space Center on January 28, 1986. *STS-107*'s launch date was close to the seventeenth anniversary of the *Challenger* tragedy. Twelve days into their mission, the members of the *STS-107 Columbia* crew marked the anniversary of the disaster with a moment of silence. Commander Husband said, "They [the *Challenger* crew] made the ultimate sacrifice, giving their lives to their country and mankind. Their dedication was an inspiration to each of us."[2]

The *Challenger* accident was only the second time in NASA's 45-year history when lives were lost. The first tragedy had occurred on January 27, 1967, during a routine flight procedure practice. While sealed in their capsule on the launchpad, Apollo 1 astronauts Virgil Grissom, Edward White, and Roger Chaffee died from asphyxiation and burns after a fire broke out in their command module.

Despite tragedies and potential dangers, there is an inexplicable wonderment about space that draws astronaut applicants to NASA by the thousands. Astronaut candidates who are selected for NASA's training program are a special breed—most are multitalented, top-of-the-class achievers with a burning curiosity and drive to experience the most life has to offer. The risks are far outweighed by the chance to explore beyond the confines of Earth. But just how safe is space flight? "In a flying machine with more than 2.5 million parts, even a 99.9 percent reliability level would still leave 2,500 things to go wrong."[3] Still, the shuttle is an amazing flying engineering feat. It blasts off like a ballistic missile connected to tanks filled with 500,000 gallons of explosive fuel, only to glide back to Earth later at the mercy of nature's own power.

COLUMBIA

Space shuttle *Columbia* was named after a small sloop that sailed out of Boston Harbor in 1787 and went on to become the first American ship to circumnavigate the world. Like its namesake, the space shuttle *Columbia* was recorded in history as NASA's shuttle orbiter fleet pioneer in space. Known as OV-102, the *Columbia* orbiter was delivered to Kennedy Space Center in Cape Canaveral, Florida, in March 1979. The space shuttle flight program began when *Columbia* lifted off on April 12, 1981.

At the time of *Columbia*'s launch, Ellen Ochoa was just finishing up work on her Master of Science degree from Stanford University in California. Ochoa became inspired to study science after attending a conference while she was an undergraduate student at San Diego State University. Ochoa had been gravitating toward a career in business or music, and had not given much thought to working in science or technology, even though she had excelled in math and science throughout her school years. "There was a conference at my college that was sponsored by the Society of Women Engineers and they were going to bring in a group of women engineers and scientists . . . and they were going to talk about what their careers were like and what their day-to-day jobs were like and that was fascinating for me, because I didn't know any scientists and engineers. I didn't really know what a career in that field meant. I didn't have any idea,"[4] said Ochoa. Although Ochoa still had many hurdles to overcome before she would get to participate in the U.S. space program, *Columbia*'s successful launch solidified a new way to travel and explore space.

Security at Kennedy Space Center and the surrounding area had been unprecedented for the launch, because of the first flight of an Israeli astronaut. Hundreds of Israelis had come to attend the launch. The countdown was going extremely well. While the countdown continued, Ochoa sat in the Operations Support Room area of the prime firing room at the Launch Control Center. As part of the MMT, which consisted of senior

THE SPACE TRANSPORTATION SYSTEM (STS)

Early on in the NASA human flight program, the astronauts' capsule was mounted on top of a rocket. When ignited, this rocket provided the lift and speed needed to get the craft into space. This type of craft was used for the Mercury, Gemini, and Apollo programs. One of the problems with this type of space-launch vehicle was that much of it was not reusable. On January 5, 1972, President Richard Nixon changed all that. He announced the launch of the shuttle program, and explained that NASA would begin to develope a reusable, low-cost space shuttle, which would include a spacecraft that could land like a plane. The first fully functional shuttle, named *Columbia*, launched on April 12, 1981. Through the end of the summer of 2006, 115 shuttles have launched, including the "Return to Flight" mission *Discovery*.

The shuttle consists of three main components: the reusable orbiter, the external fuel tank, and two booster rockets. The fuel tank and booster rockets are jettisoned during the shuttle's ascent flight. At liftoff, the gross weight of the shuttle is 4.5 million pounds (2 million kilograms), almost four times as heavy as the heaviest plane ever built. However, when the orbiter returns to Earth, it weighs only 230,000 pounds (104,326 kilograms).

government and contract managers, Ochoa and the others were "charged with reporting any issues that may affect the safety or success of the countdown or mission. Reportable issues can originate during any phase of the preflight hardware component processing as well as during the countdown itself. All issues raised must be resolved prior to clearing the launch vehicle for flight."[5]

The *STS-107* crew was in the orbiter of the shuttle. At 9:18 A.M., the signal was given to close the hatch. *STS-107* mission personnel at Kennedy Space Center and Mission Control at the Johnson Space Center in Houston went over their own checklists in preparation for a successful shuttle countdown and liftoff. Both centers were busy, because as soon as the space shuttle lifts off the launchpad in Florida, Mission Control in Houston takes command of the mission.

A DEADLY BLOW

January 16, 2003, was a beautiful day at Cape Canaveral, with nothing but clear blue skies as far as the eye could see. It was what NASA personnel call a perfect day for a shuttle launch. After a flawless countdown, *Columbia* roared off the launchpad on time at 10:39 A.M. Eastern Standard Time. The launch seemed flawless, but it had not been. On Friday, January 17, while viewing video footage that had been recorded during the launch on the previous day, NASA officials saw that a relatively large chunk of foam insulation from the giant external fuel tank had struck *Columbia*'s left wing. Ron Dittemore, manager of the space shuttle program, later stated, "We spent a goodly amount of time reviewing the film [of the launch] and analyzing what that might do. From our experience it was determined that the event did not represent a safety concern."[6] By the time the foam strike was noticed, Ellen Ochoa had already returned to Houston.

The issue nagged at NASA personnel enough that they wondered if the foam strike on the wing could have made *Columbia* vulnerable to problems in space and during reentry to Earth's atmosphere. If the foam did harm the shuttle, had

Space Shuttle Program Manager Ron Dittemore explains what happened to *Columbia* during reentry into the earth's atmosphere at a press conference on February 3, 2003, at the Johnson Space Center in Houston, Texas. Commander Rick Husband, Pilot William McCool, Flight Engineer Kalpana Chawla, Payload Commander Michael Anderson, Payload Specialist Ilan Ramon, and mission specialists Laurel Clark and David Brown were killed during the tragic accident.

any damage been done to the heat-absorbing tiles that protect the spacecraft from the intense heat of reentry? Could the foam strike set off a domino effect of peeling tiles, leaving *Columbia* unprotected in some critical area on the shuttle body? *Columbia* couldn't dock with the International Space Station (ISS), because the ship did not have the needed docking collar onboard. In addition, the *Columbia* crew was not trained in docking maneuvers, or to perform a space walk outside the shuttle to assess the potential damage (nor did they have the materials necessary to attempt a repair).

THE FATEFUL FINAL MORNING

The 16-day mission itself went well. The seven astronauts conducted their experiments and enjoyed their time in space. On the morning of February 1, 2003, the crewmembers of *Columbia* began their day listening to the song *Scotland the Brave* being piped over the radio. The song was being played for mission specialist Laurel Clark, a doctor from Iowa. Some members of Clark's family were worried about her safety. To reassure them, Clark e-mailed them about how beautiful Mount Fuji and the Sahara Desert appeared from space.

On the ground at the Kennedy Space Center, where *Columbia* was due to land sometime after 9:00 A.M., both KSC and Mission Control teams were monitoring the weather for *Columbia*'s reentry. There weren't any weather problems anywhere on the planet. Ellen Ochoa was at Mission Control in Houston to watch *Columbia*'s return. At 8:15 A.M. Eastern time, *Columbia* was given the signal to perform the de-orbit burn (a braking maneuver that brings the shuttle back to Earth). Commander Rick Husband fired the main engines to slow down the shuttle as he turned it headfirst and belly forward to deflect the intense heat that occurred during reentry. Approximately 30 minutes later, 122,000 miles (196,340 kilometers) above Hawaii, the notorious reentry glow that turns bright pink and then blinding white started to envelop the ship as atmospheric friction caused the outside temperatures to rise between 750°F and 3,000°F (399°C and 1,649°C).

At 8:56 A.M., NASA noticed an increase in brakewell and tire temperature on the sensor monitors, before they stopped transmitting data. Barely two minutes later, three sensors that had been transmitting data from the left side of the shuttle also stopped. At 8:59 A.M., capsule communicator (CAPCOM) Charlie Hobaugh alerted the crew about the tire pressure message. Aboard the shuttle, Rick Husband only managed to respond with a "Roger" before Hobaugh heard Husband say, "Uh," and then his voice was replaced by static. All of *Columbia*'s data transmissions ceased. Hobaugh tried to hail

Columbia several times but got no response. Soon after, a loud boom was heard in the skies over Nacogdoches, Texas, and debris began to rain down throughout an area that stretched from eastern Texas to Louisiana.

Within minutes of losing communication with the shuttle, NASA personnel at Mission Control in Houston knew that something had gone horribly wrong. The stunned NASA narrator was left to say, "Obviously a major malfunction."[7] A Space Shuttle contingency was declared at Mission Control in Houston. The shuttle was scheduled to land at 9:16 A.M., but never arrived.

At the MCC, it was now Ellen Ochoa's gut-wrenching task to turn to the Contingency Action Plan. In the event of any mishap, the role of the deputy director of FCOD is to assist the director, "providing overall guidance for personnel in the FCOD Action Centers, in making decisions involving the flight crew and their immediate families, and in the assignment of FCOD personnel to support the mishap investigation teams."[8]

Within hours of the loss of communication with *Columbia* and its crew, NASA began to receive a flood of calls about parts of the shuttle being found in people's backyards, on roadways, and in wooded areas throughout Texas and Louisiana. The arduous task ahead for those assigned to the *STS-107* mission was to secure as much of the shuttle wreckage as possible, recover any physical remains of *Columbia*'s crew, and begin the long, difficult job of piecing together data and debris to determine the cause of the tragedy. For Ochoa and the other members of the tight-knit NASA family, it would be a time to grieve the loss of their colleagues and friends, and then get back to work with a focus on one goal: to safely resume human space flight missions as soon as possible.

Dawn of the
Space Age

For as long as the human quest for knowledge has been recorded, things beyond the reaches of Earth have been written about with a heightened curiosity and fascination. In the Book of Genesis in the Bible, the creation of the "heavens" and Earth is described in vivid detail. When the blue-colored daylight sky gives way to the blackness of night, the sky is filled with millions of twinkles of light dotting the darkness. For centuries, people have attempted to make sense of what they saw overhead each night. The night sky has been written about in strictly scientific terms, as well as in poetry. The mystery of those twinkling lights was eventually solved, in the most scientific of terms: They are merely balls of gases, held together by their own gravity. Located millions of miles away, with a lifespan ranging from a million years to several billion years, these sparkles of light are called "stars."

ASTRONOMY AND ITS SCHOLARS

Along the way, stars were arranged in groups, called constella-tions, to make some sense of their apparent randomness. The night sky was an infinite canvas on which people, using their imagination, could project the actions and embodiments of the divine. It was a way to tell a story before the written word. As astronomer writer Ian Ridpath noted: "Constella-tions are the invention of human imagination, not of nature . . . for navigators beyond sight of land or for travelers in the track-less desert who wanted signposts, for farmers who wanted a calendar and for shepherds who wanted a nightly clock, the division of the sky into recognizable star groupings had prac-tical purposes."9

The most recognized constellation is Ursa Major, which includes the stars of the Big Dipper. If you look closely, you can see the handle of the dipper, known as the Great Bear's tail, and the cup part, which is the Bear's side. The brightest star in the Big Dipper—Polaris, or the North Star—has been used through the ages as a navigation marker for sailing ships. Even slaves escaping to freedom on the Underground Railroad described the North Star in songs.

Many of the constellations in the night sky were named after characters from Greek mythology. Perseus, son of Zeus, killed the Gorgon Medusa and rescued Andromeda from a sea monster; Orion the Hunter faces off against a raging bull; the bird Phoenix would live for 500 years before being consumed by the fire of the noon sun, only to rise from the ashes and become a bird once again.

The science of studying outer space, including celestial bodies, is called astronomy. The people who study this science are called astronomers. Throughout history, astronomers, including Hipparchus, Nicolaus Copernicus, and Galileo Galilei, have contributed to the study of the universe beyond Earth. Galileo invented the first astronomical telescope and confirmed Copernicus's theory that the planets in our solar system (a system of planets or other bodies orbiting a star) revolved around our star, the sun. After Galileo pointed his telescope toward the sky in 1610, the universe was never the same. Since that first experience seeing views of the sun, Mercury, Venus, Mars, Jupiter, Saturn, and Earth's own satellite, the moon, the quest to explore space has never stopped. Hundreds of years would pass before human space flight became a reality. In the meantime, the exploration of the universe would find its expression through people's imaginations, filling pages of fantasy writing called science fiction.

AN UNCANNY VISION

Earth's closest space neighbor is its satellite—the moon. People have watched the moon's shape change each month, going from a full glowing orb to a crescent, and then seeming to disappear into the darkness. Some people said they saw a face on the moon and that it seemed to be smiling down on Earth. Others saw craters and dark areas on the moon's surface and wondered what it was really like up there. Was it habitable? Was there life on the moon? The quest to answer those questions drove scientists and creative people from other fields to come up with some ideas. Potential answers came first through science fiction and fantasy. It would be some time before technology would catch up with the creativity of fiction.

Two science-fiction novels—*From the Earth to the Moon* (1865) and its sequel, *Round the Moon* (1870)—were written by French novelist Jules Verne nearly 100 years before NASA astronauts Frank Borman, James Lovell, and William Anders made their historic space flight around the moon on Christmas Eve, 1968. In a perfect example of real life imitating fiction, NASA's launch of *Apollo 8* eerily parallels Verne's stories about space travel.

SPACE HEROES IN TELEVISION AND FILM

Aside from books and radio, science-fiction adventures made their way into the popular imagination by way of two other technologies—motion pictures and television. Flash Gordon, which began as a comic strip in the newspaper, was re-created for the big screen in three serial installments—*Flash Gordon, Flash Gordon's Trip To Mars*, and *Flash Gordon Conquers the Universe*—between 1936 and 1940. In 1939, a 12-part movie serial depicted the adventures of *Buck Rogers* in the twenty-fifth century. *Captain Video and His Video Rangers*, which debuted on June 27, 1949, was the first science-fiction/space adventure show to air on television. Weaved into stories about "good science" versus "evil science," it also offered introductions to a variety of technological inventions, including the Opticon Scillometer; a long-range, X-ray machine that allowed its user to see through walls; the Discatron, which had a portable TV screen and doubled as an intercom; a Cosmic Ray Vibrator, which Captain Video used to paralyze his target; and an Electronic Strait Jacket, which placed captured enemies in invisible restraints. Kids throughout the country wanted to own one or more of these cool "futuristic" gadgets.

SPUTNIK

On October 4, 1957, the Soviet newspaper *Pravda* stunned the world with a report that confirmed the successful launch of a satellite into orbit around Earth. A giant rocket lifted off from its launchpad at the Baikonur Cosmodrome (in what is today Kazakhstan) carrying a small aluminum sphere under its protective cone. *Sputnik 1* (*Sputnik* is Russian for "traveler") was only 22.8 inches (57.9 centimers) in diameter, and weighed slightly over 183 pounds (83 kilograms). Once in orbit, *Sputnik 1* began to transmit an audible beeping signal from the four antenna mounted on its exterior. Those beeps, heard around the world, announced that the Soviet Union—not the United States—had successfully launched the first artificial satellite from Earth. If the Soviets could put a satellite into orbit, how long would it be before a Soviet spacecraft would be circling above and spying on Earth's inhabitants below? At this time, the United States and Soviet Union were in a race to develop missile systems capable of carrying nuclear warheads to pro-

The unmanned Soviet satellite *Sputnik 1* became the first spacecraft to orbit the earth when it was launched on October 4, 1957. Here, *Sputnik 1* is on display at the 1958 World's Fair in Brussels, Belgium.

tect their own lands against an enemy. Even before the launch of *Sputnik*, Americans found themselves looking up at the night sky, finding real reason to fear a potential Soviet threat to their freedom and safety.

Senator Lyndon B. Johnson had been hosting one of his famous barbecues at his Texas ranch on the evening the news broke about *Sputnik 1*. During a stroll later that night, he looked up at the dark sky overhead and felt as unsettled as many other Americans that evening, wondering what the Soviet success might mean for the rest of the world. He later wrote, "You learn to live closely with the sky. But now, somehow, in some new way, the sky seemed almost alien. I . . . remember the profound shock of realizing that it might be possible for another nation to achieve technological superiority over this great country of ours."[10] The United States needed to move on with its own space program, and it needed to do so quickly.

President Dwight D. Eisenhower—pictured here with Dr. T. Keith Glernan (right), the first administrator of NASA, and Dr. Hugh L. Dryden (left), the deputy administrator of NASA—officially created the National Aeronautics and Space Administration (NASA) on July 29, 1958. The government agency was established for the express purpose of building the U.S. space program and conducting civilian and military aerospace research.

THE SPACE RACE

The National Aeronautics and Space Administration (NASA) began the business of space flight and exploration just five months after Ellen Ochoa was born in 1958. Ochoa's parents could never have imagined back then that their infant daughter would one day be part of NASA's human space flight program.

NASA was created out of the old National Advisory Committee for Aeronautics (NACA). Established in 1915, the NACA was the brainchild of Charles Doolittle Walcott, head of the Smithsonian Institution in Washington, D.C. Concerned about America's lack of aeronautics superiority, Walcott received congressional approval for the creation of a research program in aerodynamics, sponsored by the federal government. "Congress gave the NACA $5000.00 for its first year of operations and charged the organization 'to supervise and direct the scientific study of the problems of flight, with a view to their practical solution.'"[11]

For the next 43 years, NACA (which included such distinguished members in the aviation field as Orville Wright, Charles A. Lindbergh, Eddie Rickenbacker, and Henry "Hap" Arnold) devoted its resources to the study of aeronautics. Its mission was to understand the behavior of aircraft in all types of flight conditions so it could make recommendations for design innovations and improvements for air flight. Thanks to the research done by NACA, the United States was better prepared for aerial combat at the outbreak of World War II (1939–1945) than it had been for World War I (1914–1918).

For those rare individuals who have no fear of the unknown, pushing the limits of flight was an exhilarating challenge. The test pilots who worked at the NACA used the skies as their laboratory, taking the latest designs in aircraft technology off into the reaches of the horizon to see what they could do. It was on the NACA experimental flight field at Muroc Dry Lake, California, on October 14, 1947, that U.S. Air Force Captain Chuck Yeager flew the Bell X-1 aircraft faster than the speed of sound. This historic flight "is generally accepted as the first supersonic flight by a piloted aircraft. Captain Yeager ignited the four-chambered XLR-11 rocket engines after being air-launched from under the bomb bay of a JTB-29A at 21,000 feet. The 6,000-pound thrust ethyl alcohol/liquid oxygen burning rockets . . . pushed him up to a speed of Mach 1.06 at an altitude of 45,000 feet."[12]

After Yeager's flight, many of the NACA staff engineers and scientists believed that flight beyond the atmosphere would eventually be achieved, though in incremental steps. The successful launch of *Sputnik 1* brought the process to the forefront of the aeronautics industry.

U.S. President Dwight D. Eisenhower was besieged by criticism when the Soviets beat the United States into orbit. Two years into his presidency, Eisenhower himself had announced that the United States would launch "history's first artificial Earth satellite some time between July, 1957 and December, 1958 as part of the International Geophysical Year."[13] As part of this yearlong event, 5,000 scientists from 40 countries would come together to study planet Earth from its ocean depths to the outer reaches of its atmosphere. America's man-made satellite would be an integral part of the research, providing detailed information about the earth from its vantage point above. Once *Sputnik 1* was in orbit, Americans not only felt threatened, but they were embarrassed by the failure of their own space program. Before the United States could even begin to catch up in the "space race," the Soviets would stun the world two more times.

On November 3, 1957, just one month after *Sputnik 1*'s historic launch, the Soviet Union sent another *Sputnik* into space, this time with a living creature aboard. *Sputnik 2*'s cargo was a dog named Laika. Laika's 10-day space flight would provide scientists with the first data on how conditions in space affected living creatures. In its rush to get an American satellite into space, the U.S. Naval Research Laboratory, assigned to build an unmanned satellite, tried to launch the *Vanguard TV-3* rocket from Cape Canaveral on December 6, 1957. On television, in full view of the world, *TV-3* lifted just inches off the ground before slamming back down onto the launchpad and exploding into a ball of flame.

After *TV-3*'s embarrassing failure, President Eisenhower tapped the talents of a German rocket scientist named Wernher von Braun. Von Braun and his team, who had been working on their own rocket launch research for German leader Adolf Hitler during World War II, had come to the United States to work with American scientists and engineers. Working at the Army Ballistic Missile Agency in Huntsville, Alabama, von Braun and his colleagues provided the lift the

United States needed. Von Braun was certain that Redstone rocket, a highly developed V-2 used during the war to bomb targets in England and Belgium, could successfully put a satellite into orbit. Under cover of darkness on the evening of January 31, 1958, von Braun's *Juno-1* lifted off at Cape Canaveral, putting the *Explorer 1* unmanned satellite into space. America's first space launch led to a great discovery: a doughnut-shaped area made up of energetic atomic particles that were circling the earth. A potential hazard for future flights with humans, the region was later named the Allen radiation belt after Dr. James van Allen, who had built the instruments that detected it.

NASA: AMERICA'S SPACE AGENCY

To streamline the efforts of the various research agencies and create the world's first civilian space program, President Eisenhower signed the National Aeronautics and Space Act on July 29, 1958. The act established the National Aeronautics and Space Administration (NASA), whose goals included sending the first American into space.

The U.S. space program was truly born with the opening of the United States' newest federal agency on the morning of October 1, 1958. With a budget of more than $100 million, 8,000 employees, and three laboratories (Langley, in Maryland; Ames, in Iowa; and Lewis, in Cleveland, Ohio), NASA was fully committed to winning the space race.

NASA launched several more satellites, including *Vanguard 2*, which provided the first photographs of Earth from space; *Tiros*, the first weather satellite; *Transit 1B*, the first navigation satellite; and *Echo 1*, the first communications satellite. All of this was achieved before the end of August 1960.

As exciting as these accomplishments were, however, the real goal was to send humans into space. NASA had its first group of astronauts already training for Project Mercury. This program was supposed to put a manned spacecraft into orbit around Earth and investigate the survival and performance of

The Mercury Seven program was established in 1959 to send a manned spacecraft into orbit around the earth. Pictured here, from left, are the Mercury Seven astronauts—Lieutenant M. Scott Carpenter, Captain L. Gordon Cooper, Colonel John H. Glenn, Jr., Captain Virgil "Gus" Grissom, Lieutenant Commander Walter Schirra, Lieutenant Commander Alan B. Shepard, Jr., and Captain Donald K. "Deke" Slayton—during training at Langley Air Force Base in Virginia.

a human being in a space environment. Mercury Seven astronauts John Glenn, Alan Shepard, Walter Schirra, Virgil Grissom, L. Gordon Cooper, Scott Carpenter, and Donald Slayton were test pilots who were chosen from among thousands of applicants to become the first Americans in space.

NASA had hoped to put the first human into space before the Soviets, despite getting a late start in the space race. But it was not to be. The Soviet Union was once again a step ahead of the United States. Russian cosmonaut (the Russian term for *astronaut*) Yuri Alexeyevich Gagarin became the first human to reach space. He made his historic 108-minute flight circling

THE FIRST WOMEN OF NASA: UNLUCKY MERCURY 13

On October 1, 1959, NASA introduced its first group of astronauts. Known as the "Mercury Seven," all of them were men, all were chosen from the military, and all were trained test pilots. Much less known is the fact that 13 women candidates passed the same physical and psychological tests that the Mercury astronauts had undergone, but were not selected to become astronauts. To avoid accusations of discrimination, NASA excluded the women by saying that astronauts were required to be qualified *test* pilots, which the women were not.

Astronaut candidates Jerrie Cobb and Janey Hart took their case to the U.S. Congress. In hearings held in July 1962 to debate what the official qualifications should be for astronauts, Cobb stated, "We seek only a place in our nation's space future without discrimination."* Committee chairman, Congressman Victor Anfuso (R-New York), revealed his own bias when he said, "I think that we can safely say at this time that the whole purpose of space exploration is to someday colonize these other planets, and I don't see how we can do that without women."**

Eventually, women would become astronauts and fly missions, beginning with the six chosen to join NASA Group 8 in 1978—Anna Lee Fisher, Shannon Lucid, Judith Resnik, Sally Ride, Margaret Seddon, and Kathryn Dwyer. Sally Ride became the first American woman in space, and Judith Resnik was the second. Anna Fisher was the first mother in space, and Shannon Lucid set the U.S. time-in-space endurance record at 188 consecutive days in orbit while aboard the Russian Mir space station.

*   Available online at *http://www.daviddarling.info/encyclopedia/M/Mercury_hirteen.html.*
** Ibid.

the earth aboard his spaceship *Vostok 1* on April 12, 1961. Human space travel was now a reality.

THE EAGLE HAS LANDED

The United States caught up with the Soviets quickly when the Mercury Redstone (MR3) rocket launch vehicle lifted the first piloted spacecraft from Cape Canaveral at 9:34 A.M. Eastern Standard Time on May 5, 1961. During his 15-minute suborbital flight aboard *Freedom 7*, astronaut Alan B. Shepard, Jr., reached an altitude of 115 nautical miles (132 miles; 213 kilometers). It was an achievement of little consequence in the eyes of many people, because Yuri Gagarin's flight had been more substantial. Determined to set America's sights higher, newly elected President John F. Kennedy addressed a joint session of Congress to talk about the space program:

> Now is the time to take longer strides. Time for a great new American enterprise—time for this nation to take a clearly leading role in space achievement, which, in many ways, may hold the key to our future on Earth. . . . I believe that this nation should commit itself to achieving the goal, before this decade is out, of landing a man on the Moon and returning him safely to the Earth.[14]

The Soviets' early glory in the space race began to give way to delays and failures, while NASA continued to move forward. NASA continued to build on its successes by establishing new programs, including Project Gemini (two-manned space capsule flights) from 1963–1966 and Project Apollo (three-manned space flights) from 1961–1975. Although President Kennedy did not live to see an American land on the moon, the feat did take place before the decade's end, as Kennedy had envisioned. Along with millions of other people, 11-year-old Ellen Ochoa watched the televised broadcast when *Apollo 11* astronaut Neil Armstrong stepped foot on the surface of the moon on July 20, 1969, and proclaimed, "That's one small

On July 20, 1969, *Apollo 11* became the first manned spacecraft to land on the moon. Mission commander Neil Armstrong took this picture of lunar module pilot Eugene "Buzz" Aldrin on the surface of the moon.

step for man, one giant leap for mankind." With the moon landing achieved, NASA set its sights on developing a spacecraft that could be launched into space aboard a rocket, and land back on Earth like an airplane. This would be the space shuttle program.

Four decades after the creation of NASA, Roger D. Launius, chief historian of NASA, said:

When future generations review the history of the twentieth century, they will undoubtedly judge humanity's movement into space, with both machines and people, as one of its seminal developments. Even at this juncture, the compelling nature of spaceflight—and the activity that it has engendered on the part of many peoples and governments—makes the U.S. civil space program a significant area of investigation. People from all avenues of experience and levels of education share an interest in the drama of spaceflight.[15]

3

Born of Two Heritages

Lauri Ellen Ochoa was born on May 10, 1958. She was the third child born to Joe and Rosanne Ochoa. Her oldest sister, Beth, was born in 1954, and her brother Monte was born in 1957. Two younger brothers, Tyler (1962) and Wilson (1964), rounded out the Ochoa clan. Ellen's father, Joe, was of Mexican descent. His family came from Sonora, the second-largest state in Mexico. Located in the northwestern part of Mexico, just below Arizona, Sonora underwent several waves of Spanish exploration after first being visited by Francisco Vásquez de Coronado in the mid-1500s. In the 1600s, Spanish missionaries were active in colonizing the territory.

The state of Sonora is situated in some of the most beautiful territory on either side of the Mexico–United States border. It has incredible natural diversity, including the Sonoran Desert, the Sea of Cortez, and the Sierra Madre mountains. Today, Sonora is important for its cattle production and mining. It is also a popular tourist attraction because of its beautiful beaches. Culturally, Sonora is the source of an unusual style of music known as Norteño, a type of traditional Mexican music that originated in the rural northern part of Mexico in the early twentieth century.

THE OCHOA FAMILY

Ellen's father, Joe, was the youngest of 12 children. Although he was not born in Mexico, he was raised in a Spanish-speaking family. Unfortunately, the Ochoas faced discrimination and many of the same prejudices that other minorities encountered when they came to the United States. This treatment left an indelible impression on Joe and impacted the way he raised his own children. In an interview, Ellen Ochoa recalled what she knew about her father and his family:

> After [Joe's parents] were married and had a few kids they immigrated to the United States, first to Arizona, then on to California. My dad was the youngest of 12, so they were already living in California when he was born. But he did grow up in a household where his parents never really did learn English, so he spoke Spanish at home and English in school. Unfortunately, though, by the time he grew up and had kids, because of some of the experiences he had when he was a child he saw English as important. He didn't feel it was important necessarily to learn Spanish or be bilingual, although my mother tried to convince him that it was important. I can remember hearing from my aunts and uncles that, for example, at the high school that they went to, there was a pool that the Hispanic kids were only allowed to use one day a week, which was the day before the cleaning crew came . . . and that my grandfather was so upset at that kind of discrimination that he wouldn't even let his kids swim in the pool at all. He said if that's their policy, we can do without it.[16]

THE DEARDORFF FAMILY

Ellen's mother, Rosanne Deardorff, grew up in an entirely different environment from that of her future husband. Born on

December 30, 1920, in Tulsa, Oklahoma, Rosanne was the fourth of five children. Her oldest brother, Wilson, was named after their mother's maiden name. Naming a male child Wilson would become a family tradition. Rosanne's oldest sister, Judy, was born next, followed by a brother named Derry. Rosanne was born after Derry, and later, youngest sister Gloria arrived.

As a child, Rosanne suffered from asthma. The condition was severe enough that a doctor advised Rosanne's parents to move to the West Coast, where the climate would ease their daughter's breathing problems. The Deardorffs moved to California, settling in Hollywood in 1935. Although the change in environment did improve Rosanne's health, she was still unable to do many things, including attending high school. The Deardorffs hired a tutor to teach their teenage daughter at home. Rosanne did not officially receive her high school equivalency diploma until she was in her 30s.

Living near Hollywood had its advantages. Rosanne and her sister Gloria filled their autograph books with the signatures of movie stars such as Clark Gable and Shirley Temple. According to Ellen, her mother and aunt were huge movie fans, and they "had their pictures taken with stars on Hollywood Boulevard."[17] While in her late teens, Rosanne got a job working as an usherette at the famous Grauman's Chinese Theater. It wasn't too long before she was promoted to other positions, eventually working her way up to executive secretary for the head of Twentieth Century Fox's West Coast Theaters. Being in the motion picture industry had its perks, and Rosanne and her sister Gloria took full advantage of the opportunity to hobknob with the great Hollywood stars of the time.

THE OCHOA CHILDREN

Ellen's parents couldn't have come from more different backgrounds. Still, the two met, fell in love, and married in 1946. After fulfilling his required tour of duty in the navy, Joe Ochoa began a career with the Los Angeles, California, division of

Ellen Ochoa's mother, Rosanne, and her family moved to Los Angeles in 1935. While she was a teenager, Rosanne worked at Grauman's Chinese Theater, which is pictured here in the 1950s.

Sears, Roebuck and Company. He and Rosanne had their first child, a daughter named Beth, in 1954. The oldest of the Ochoa clan, Beth is now an attorney in the entertainment industry. In 1957, their first son, Monte, was born. Today, he is an instructional media specialist in the San Diego city schools and has a private pilot's license.

About a year after Ellen was born in 1958, the growing Ochoa family moved from Los Angeles to La Mesa, California, after Joe was promoted to superintendent of the Sears San Diego store. In 1962, Ellen's younger brother Tyler was born.

Today, Tyler is a law professor at Santa Clara University. Rosanne and Joe's last child arrived in 1964. Youngest brother Wilson is now the principal music librarian of the Nashville Symphony in Tennessee.

EDUCATION IS KEY

The Ochoa children were always encouraged to apply themselves in school and take part in extracurricular activities. Rosanne instilled the importance of a solid education in her children from the time they were very young. Having always been interested in learning, Rosanne began taking college courses when Ellen was just one year old. Because of her family responsibilities, Rosanne could not take many classes each semester, but that didn't stop her from pursuing her love of learning. She took one class each semester at San Diego State University over a span of 22 years, and in June 1982, she graduated with a 3.9 grade point average. Ellen says her mother's focus wasn't on finishing college as much as it was on the sheer enjoyment of learning. That left an indelible impression on Ellen throughout her school years.

Rosanne also introduced her children to the arts and supported each child's desire to cultivate hobbies. "We were all encouraged to do whatever we wanted to do,"[18] says Ellen. Reading was always one of Ellen's favorite pastimes, so it's not surprising that she recalls one particular book, *A Wrinkle in Time,* as a favorite from her elementary school days.

Could Ellen have known at such a young age that she wanted to be an astronaut? As a child, she certainly kept abreast of some of the milestones reached by NASA. While she was growing up, American astronauts were circling the earth as part of the Mercury Program. NASA then sent astronauts farther into space, with the flight crew of *Apollo 8* successfully traveling around the moon. All of these astronauts were men. Ellen never read about any female astronauts, because there *were* no female astronauts in the NASA program until the time Ellen Ochoa was 20 years old. Ochoa later said,

Young Ellen Ochoa was always interested in space exploration. She followed news of NASA missions such as *Apollo 8*. Pictured here is the *Apollo 8* team of Commander Frank Borman, Command Module Pilot James Lovell (center), and Lunar Module Pilot William Anders (rear), as they prepare to head to the launchpad on December 21, 1968.

When those first six women were selected to the astronaut corps in 1978, I clipped that article out of the paper and I wasn't even thinking about being an astronaut at that point. It was a big deal, and you thought "well, now that's something people can dream of doing that you couldn't before." People often ask me, did you grow up dreaming or aiming to become an astronaut? And my answer is, of course not, because nobody ever asked you that question. Women were totally excluded. There was no teacher or anybody out there who would say well, gosh, you do well in math, you could grow up to become an astronaut.[19]

Because there were no women in the U.S. space program (unlike the Soviet Union, which sent Valentina Tereshkova into space in 1963), it didn't occur to Ellen to think of becoming an astronaut when she was a child. Since there were few female scientists at all, Ellen didn't think about pursuing a career in the sciences or engineering, both essential disciplines for astronaut candidates.

ROSANNE'S INFLUENCE

There was no shortage of extracurricular pursuits to consider in the Ochoa family. Because Rosanne had wanted to take music lessons as a child but never got to do so, she really wanted her children to have that opportunity. Music became an integral part of all their lives. Beth chose the clarinet, Monte played the saxophone, Ellen played the flute, and Wilson chose the French horn. According to Wilson, all five Ochoa kids also played the piano and were part of band programs all the way through high school.

All five Ochoa children knew how their mother felt about the importance of education. In an interview, Wilson Ochoa recalled how his mother always found interesting ways to make learning a part of their family time: "We had reference books around the house and we played games at the dinner table . . . we played this geography game where she'd get out a map and somebody would pick a place and the rest of us had to guess where it was. She had flash cards, and we were always playing games . . . and it was a very good childhood. We all enjoyed playing games together."[20]

Rosanne was proud of her children and their accomplishments. Wilson also recalled that when the Ochoa children were contemplating career choices, Rosanne joked that she hoped one of them would grow up to become a doctor, one would be a dentist, and one would be a lawyer, so that when she got old, she would have "all of her services taken care of." Wilson said, "She was proud of the fact that she had given us a chance to sample all sorts of different things as kids and we had found what made us rich, what made us happy. . . . It was that kind of love of learning that my mother instilled in us that led us on the paths that we all found, and I think she was proud of that. . . . She used to tell everyone that she had a kid in every time zone, and she thought that was kind of cool."[21]

A MAJOR CHANGE

Rosanne's impact on her children's lives became even more apparent when the Ochoas marriage ended in 1970. According to Wilson, Joe's departure was abrupt: "We really never saw him after that. He all of a sudden changed and didn't want to be married and didn't want a family, and just wanted out and just left."[22] Joe's departure left Rosanne to raise five children between the ages of 6 and 16 on her own. It would be a challenge for all of the Ochoas to face and would reveal both Rosanne's strength and determination and the Ochoa children's resiliency and spirit.

4

Without Limits

Joe Ochoa's absence from the family was a major change in the lives of his five children, but with the love and guidance from their mother, Ellen and her siblings lived as normal a life as possible. Rosanne, the Ochoa children say, was an incredible woman. "The amount of energy it would take to be there for all five of us and to drive us to music lessons and go to school functions and make sure we were all doing well in school, it's truly remarkable,"[23] says Wilson.

Staying connected to family was extremely important to Rosanne, and she made sure the children spent time with her own family as well as the relatives of her estranged husband. The children also got some exposure to their Hispanic culture when they visited the Ochoa clan, headed by Joe's mother, whom the children fondly called "Mama Grande." There was the paella party—which focused on cooking a traditional Spanish meal of rice, meat, and seafood in a huge pan outdoors all day. Vacations were spent driving to visit friends and relatives who lived in other parts of the country. There were frequent trips back to Oklahoma, where Rosanne still had family.

There is no doubt that Rosanne's love of education had a positive influence on her children. Monte and Ellen were closest in age and they helped each other through their father's absence. To cope with the change, they threw themselves even more deeply than usual into their schoolwork. Ellen enjoyed school, and did well in her classes. In fact, all the Ochoa children excelled in school. Many of them even had the same teachers, but they were not competitive with each other. Wilson says, "[W]e were all real successful in school, and the temptation might be to compare grades and stuff like that but it wasn't that way. I think we just all expected of ourselves to get good grades."[24]

Although Ellen hadn't really settled into a preference for one particular subject over another, she did like math. She spent her grade school days attending Northmont Elementary School in La Mesa. Ellen fondly remembers the fifth grade. That year, her class was divided up into groups to form their own "countries" as part of a yearlong social studies project. Each "country" was assigned to form a type of government of their choosing. Ellen recalled:

It was a little bit different that year from my other years in school. We competed all year long with other countries on various projects. Sometimes at the end of the day, we would have debates with the other groups, for which you could win points for your country. I remember being more interested in school that year than other years. It was fun having the freedom to pick our own topics for research. It was a very creative year.[25]

Despite the breakup of her parents' marriage, Ellen continued to excel in all her endeavors. When she was 13, she moved from elementary school to junior high school, attending Parkway Middle School. While there, she won the San Diego

Ellen Ochoa grew up in the San Diego area and attended San Diego State University. Pictured here is the skyline of the Southern California city from San Diego Bay.

spelling bee, and in seventh and eighth grade, she was named Outstanding Student at Parkway. Living with her mom and four siblings provided a solid emotional support system for the blossoming teen.

A BUDDING FLUTIST

Besides education, Ellen's other passion was music. Her choice was the transverse flute, a woodwind instrument that dates back to the Middle Ages. As a public school student, Ellen played the flute in school bands and wind ensembles from sixth grade through high school, and was touted as a top performer. She was so talented, in fact, that while she was still in high school she auditioned and was asked to play the flute with the Civic Youth Orchestra in San Diego. Ellen became such an accomplished flutist that she continued to play in college, and while she was a graduate student at Stanford University, she won the Student Soloist Award for the Stanford Symphony Orchestra.

ACADEMIC EXCELLENCE

Ellen Ochoa made the transition from junior high school to high school with ease. At Grossmont High School, she quickly became one of the best math students, which was unusual for girls at the time. During an interview with *La Prensa San Diego*, Ochoa later explained that girls just weren't encouraged to consider majoring in math and science once they got to college. Ochoa, however, was fortunate to have a calculus teacher, Ms. Paz Jensen, who made math an engaging subject and inspired her to continue studying math in college.

Ochoa credits many of her teachers at Grossmont with helping her learn by making school enjoyable and exciting. Ochoa especially enjoyed her English classes. She says teachers Jeanne Dorsey and Dani Barton provided a learning atmosphere where interaction was an important component of class time. All of Ochoa's hard work and determination culminated in a prestigious honor. At the end of her senior year, she was named the valedictorian (top student) of her 1975 graduating class.

STAYING CLOSE TO HOME

Ellen Ochoa had seen the sacrifices Rosanne had made for her children and had reaped the intangible rewards of her mother's encouragement and support throughout her youth. Now she wanted to help her mother continue to instill those precious ideals in her younger brothers. Getting a good education had been the paramount lesson, and Ochoa wanted all her siblings to receive good educations. So, instead of going away for college, Ochoa decided to attend San Diego State University to pursue her college education. This choice would allow her to remain close to her family to provide whatever support and encouragement to her siblings she could.

When Ochoa began her studies at San Diego State, she started to think about a major and a future career. Unfortunately, at that time, she didn't have as many female role models as students do today. "[I] think when I was growing up in middle and high school they weren't terribly worried about bringing in role models, especially for girls or minorities,"[26] Ochoa said. At first, Ochoa thought about a career in music or business. Despite her love of music, however, Ochoa realized that she wanted a more secure future, and music is often an unstable and risky profession. Still, she didn't know where to focus her energies. She knew she loved math, and she took math classes for fun instead of to fulfill an academic requirement. Ochoa had observed that the other math students had some recognition that the equations they were solving were connected to the physical world. Ochoa wanted to learn more.

THE SCIENCE OF NATURE

It was only after changing her major five times that Ochoa decided to major in physics, thanks to a professor who encouraged her to try it after she had done well in one of his classes. Physics is the study of matter, energy, motion, and force. The word *physics* comes from the Greek language, meaning "the science of nature."

Physics was a tough field of study, but Ochoa was up to the challenge. "I found my niche then," says Ochoa. "In my undergraduate days at SDSU, I explored several majors before choosing physics. But when I took a physics class for non-majors, it grabbed my interest so fast that I wanted to find out how to apply math to a scientific field."[27]

Majoring in physics opened doors to potential careers that Ochoa hadn't even thought about before. Her physics department advisor told Ochoa that physics majors were much sought after by employers, because a physics education helps develop very desirable skills, including abstract thinking and problem solving. People with physics degrees have a number of interesting career paths in a variety of disciplines, from education to research to optics and electronics. Even at this point, however, the idea of becoming an astronaut hadn't quite entered Ochoa's mind.

As an undergraduate, Ochoa also hadn't really considered continuing her studies in graduate school. That changed when she took a summer job working at a national research laboratory. Ochoa took note of the fact that the people there who had

FAMOUS PHYSICISTS AND THEIR CONTRIBUTIONS TO SCIENCE

Physics is a science that deals with matter and energy and their interactions. The desire to understand the fascinating universe we live in has led many men and women to study physics. In some cases, this study has led to great discoveries and inventions that remain in use today.

In 1769, Scottish physicist James Watt discovered that, by condensing steam in a separate vessel within an engine, he could make the engine faster and more fuel-efficient. The creation of the modern steam engine is considered the starting point of the Industrial Revolution. In 1857, Frenchman Jean-Bernard-León Foucault accurately measured the speed of light and invented the Foucault pendulum, using it to prove that the earth rotates on its axis. In 1895, German-born physicist Wilhelm Röntgen produced the world's first "X-ray" photograph, which showed the bones of his wife's hand. The following year, French scientist Antoine-Henri Becquerel, with colleagues Pierre Curie and Marie Curie, discovered radioactivity, which ultimately led to the medical use of radioactive substances in treating serious illnesses such as cancer.

Perhaps one of the most significant creations born out of the field of physics is a weapon that threatens the continued existence of humankind—the atomic bomb. Along with several other internationally recognized distinguished scientists, Hungarian-born nuclear physicist Edward Teller was enlisted to work on the top-secret Manhattan Project and became known as the "Father of the hydrogen bomb." This dangerous weapon was ultimately used to help bring an end to World War II.

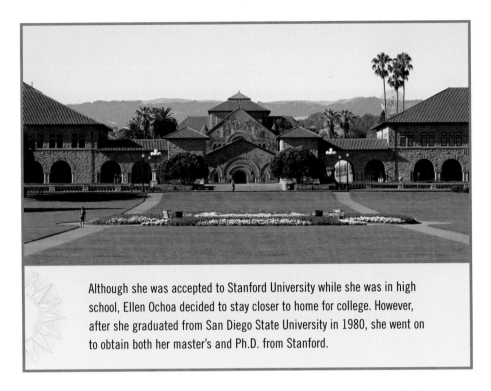

Although she was accepted to Stanford University while she was in high school, Ellen Ochoa decided to stay closer to home for college. However, after she graduated from San Diego State University in 1980, she went on to obtain both her master's and Ph.D. from Stanford.

advanced degrees were the ones who got to make all the research decisions. She also thought they got to do most of the interesting work. In a later speech, Ochoa mentioned a conversation she had with one of the staff members back then that helped set her on a course for graduate school and beyond: "[The only woman in the group] encouraged me to consider grad school and even gave me the name of a world-renowned professor at Stanford as a possible thesis advisor."[28] That Stanford professor was Dr. Joseph W. Goodman. A few years after Ochoa had this talk with her coworker, she was working with Dr. Goodman in the field of optical processing.

ON TO STANFORD

In the spring of 1980, Ochoa graduated from San Diego State at the top of her class, earning her Bachelor of Science degree in physics. Her scholastic excellence caught the attention of post-graduate institutions, and Stanford was among them. This time, Ochoa did not waiver in her choice. She decided to pursue her graduate work at Stanford University. Ochoa was comfortable with Stanford for many reasons, besides the fact that it was one of the best-rated educational institutions in the country. Ochoa was looking for a university with a diverse student body and a school that offered a wide range of courses and departments in both the sciences *and* the arts. She had not abandoned her love of music, and she wanted to attend a graduate school where she could continue to pursue this interest. Stanford met all of her requirements.

When she was accepted at Stanford to continue her studies in the sciences, Ochoa still had not thought about applying to the astronaut program at NASA. However, being a part of Stanford's educational environment opened up more career choices than Ochoa could have imagined. It would only be a matter of time before she was thinking about a career in space exploration.

5

Studying to Become an Astronaut

Ellen Ochoa began her graduate studies at Stanford in the fall of 1980. Her younger brothers were teenagers now, and Ochoa was more comfortable going away to school. Stanford University was more than 400 miles from her hometown of La Mesa, California.

Stanford University has a long and prestigious history in the world of academia. The school's motto—"The wind of freedom blows"—exemplifies the philosophy at Stanford: Both students and faculty members have the freedom to openly pursue their interests in research and teaching. As Ochoa took her first steps on campus in the fall of 1980, she had the benefit of the school's 104-year history and the legacy of those students and teachers who had come before her.

ELECTRICAL ENGINEERING

From the time Ochoa had attended a conference at San Diego State that included guest speakers from the Society of Women Engineers,

45

the field of engineering had intrigued her. Although she had been discouraged from pursuing a course of study in the discipline by a male advisor as an undergraduate because it was "difficult," there were no words of discouragement voiced by anyone at Stanford. Ochoa loved math and excelled at it, and she wanted to put those skills to use.

Electrical engineering deals with the study of electricity and electromagnetism. It is an expansive field that includes many subfields, such as control systems, electronics, and telecommunications. As she worked toward her Master of Science degree, Ochoa had the opportunity to develop her own program of study with the assistance of a faculty advisor.

A Mentor in Optical Processes

Ochoa had begun to take an interest in the study of optics—a science that deals with light—while at San Diego State University. There was a wide array of courses at Stanford that she could include in her studies. Ochoa had also developed an interest in a mathematical technique called Fourier transforms—an operation that converts functions from time to frequency domains. For example, if you played the musical note middle C, a musician with perfect pitch could tell you that your note was indeed middle C. Some well-trained musicians can even identify individual notes when more than one is being played at a time, like a chord on a piano or guitar. However, this process becomes more difficult when more notes are played simultaneously. People may not be able to hear which frequencies are being played, but a Fourier transform can.

While Ochoa was an undergraduate student, her academic advisor had given her the name of a world-renowned professor who could serve as her advisor at Stanford. His name was Joseph W. Goodman. As a distinguished faculty member in the electrical engineering department at Stanford, Goodman spent many years studying and researching physical optics. He even wrote a textbook on the subject called *Introduction to Fourier Optics*. He has received many honors and awards for his work in the field of optics, including the F. E. Terman Award of the American Society for Engineering Education and the 1990 Frederick Ives Medal, the highest award presented by the Optical Society of America. Ochoa took a class with Goodman and did so well that he began to work with her on research problems. Goodman said of Ochoa, "It soon became clear that Ellen was incredibly well organized and extremely competent with both theory and experiment."[29]

With professors like Goodman encouraging Ochoa to study electrical engineering, she continued to excel in her academic career. Ochoa completed the university requirements for her graduate degree in 1981. She was awarded a Master of Science degree in electrical engineering. Now she had to decide what she would do next.

Doctoral Studies in Optics

Even though she had not taken a break in her schooling since she started kindergarten, Ochoa immediately moved on to begin her studies toward earning her Ph.D. in electrical engineering. She chose to specialize in designing optical systems that analyze and make decisions about the objects they "see." Continuing to study under Dr. Goodman, Ochoa began working on her thesis. In academia, a thesis is a written document that conveys the research and findings of the student. An examining committee made up of members of the faculty reviews the thesis and asks the student questions to test his or her knowledge of the subject matter.

The first research paper Ochoa coauthored with Goodman was entitled *Ray Directions in Speckle Patterns*. Goodman described it as "an esoteric subject but one of some interest to a group of people in optics. . . . Her thesis research was jointly supervised by myself and Professor Lambertus Hesselink, and involved a new technique for detecting very small defects in periodic patterns, using real-time holography. . . . The experiments were quite sophisticated, and Ellen carried them out with great skill."[30] While working on her doctorate, Ochoa specialized in designing optical systems that analyzed and drew conclusions about the objects they "saw." Ochoa developed an optical system designed to

A CIRCLE OF FRIENDS

TEACHERS SERVE ELLEN OCHOA WELL

Throughout her educational training, Ellen Ochoa excelled in her studies. While in high school, she was influenced by many of her teachers. Paz Jensen, Ochoa's calculus teacher, had made math such an engaging subject for the teen that she elected to continue her math studies when she entered college at San Diego State University. A solid foundation in both math and science prepared Ochoa to enter the astronaut program. Aside from the specific influence her math teacher may have had on her, Ochoa simply loved to learn and two of her English literature teachers—Jeanne Dorsey and Dani Barton—created an atmosphere where interaction was a key component of the learning process. All three teachers had an early influence on shaping Ochoa's career by instilling a cooperative, interactive learning environment.

When Ochoa wanted to pursue a career in electrical engineering, particularly focusing on optical information processing, it was Stanford professor Joseph W. Goodman who provided the educational mentorship. Goodman was renowned for his work and research in Fourier Optics, and was also very supportive of women who wanted to study electrical engineering. According to Ochoa, approximately 10 percent of the students in the graduate school for electrical engineering at Stanford were women and she was one of only a handful of women in Goodman's research group. Among these female students was Christina Johnson, who today is the Dean of the School of Engineering at Duke University.

detect imperfections in repeating patterns. This invention was later patented in 1987. Today, it can be used for quality control in the manufacturing of various complex parts.

In later years, Ochoa explained her graduate school research in more detail:

Ochoa also counts among her influences the 18 Stanford alumni who went on to become members of the NASA astronaut corps. "There had been a number of astronauts already from Stanford, and of course Sally Ride had already been selected by the time I got to Stanford and there had been astronauts previous to that—Owen Garriott who had flown on Skylab. To be in a place where people have done that, it makes it seem a lot more possible and a lot more real."*

Today, Ochoa's best friends are people in the astronaut corps, and she feels that one of the most rewarding aspects of her job is getting the chance to work closely with so many incredibly talented people—people from a vast array of backgrounds, even different countries—all of whom share the common goal of creating a seamless operating team permeated "with a degree of camaraderie and friendship that is hard to explain."**

One cannot talk about Ochoa's influences without including her mother, Rosanne. Through hard work, determination, and perseverance, Rosanne was a catalyst for instilling in her children the importance of getting a good education and pursuing their goals. When considering a career as an astronaut, Ochoa sensed that NASA was looking for candidates who had those qualities. With Rosanne providing the support for her daughter to flourish, the influence from teachers and colleagues, and Ochoa's own hard work, determination, and perseverance, she has become a terrific role model for the next generation of scientists, engineers, astronauts, musicians, and artists yet to come.

* Interview conducted with Ellen Ochoa by author on February 4, 2005.
** Ibid.

While I was at Stanford and while I was working before becoming an astronaut, I was involved in doing research in equipment like lasers and holograms. Maybe you've seen some demonstrations of a laser or holograms either at your school or in a museum. And we were looking at those specifically for processing images—for example, trying to find a particular object within an image. You might use that on a manufacturing line if you're trying to inspect equipment and you're looking for defects; or you might use it on an autonomous lander to Mars when you're trying to land around a particular spot and you're using a video camera to look for it. And you can use optics to help you find the right place. Those were the kinds of things I was looking at and those were what some of my patents are in.[31]

DEVELOPING A CAREER PATH

Ochoa graduated from Stanford in 1985 with a Ph.D. in electrical engineering. Although she had not seriously thought about a career as an astronaut before entering graduate school, that all changed after she began her studies at Stanford. She later explained, "It was when I was at Stanford that I heard about the astronaut program, from some friends who were applying. I had never considered it before because it never occurred to me that I would get to a position in my life where I might be qualified. But when I wrote and found out the basic qualifications were a college degree in science and engineering, which I had, and either work experience or a graduate degree which I was in the process of getting, I realized that I was at least eligible to apply."[32]

After she earned her doctorate, Ochoa filled out an application for the astronauts candidates program and sent it in to NASA, but felt she had very little chance of being selected. Instead, she focused her energies on looking for a job where she could continue to do research work in optical information processing. She found that opportunity at Sandia National Laboratories, a government-owned agency with locations at

STANFORD UNIVERSITY ALUMNI

Ellen Ochoa gave up a four-year undergraduate degree scholarship from Stanford so she could be closer to her family and help her mother with younger siblings Tyler and Wilson. However, when Stanford accepted her application to pursue graduate studies in electrical engineering, Ochoa joined the list of the many distinguished artists, writers, journalists, scientists, politicians, and athletes who have pursued and graduated with degrees from this prestigious university.

Among the well-known Stanford alumni are former Supreme Court Justice Sandra Day O'Connor, U.S. senators Max Baucus (D-MT) and Jeff Bingaman (D-NM), writer John Steinbeck, actors Ted Danson and Sigourney Weaver, and athletes Tiger Woods, John McEnroe, and John Elway. Stanford also has had 18 former students who went on to pursue careers in the space program.

In 1965, Owen Garriott, became the first graduate of Stanford to serve as an astronaut. He was the science-pilot for *Skylab-3 (SL-3)*, the second manned Skylab mission, and as mission specialist on *STS-9/Spacelab*, which carried the first international shuttle crew into space. Sally Ride, who earned four educational degrees from Stanford, was one of the first six women astronauts selected by NASA. She became the first American woman in space when she was part of the crew of *STS-7* in 1983 and is the only person to serve on both of the panels investigating shuttle accidents (*Challenger* explosion and *Columbia* disaster). Mae Jemison, the first African-American female in space, joined NASA in 1987. Jemison was just 16 years old when she entered Stanford as a freshman.

When Ochoa was selected as an astronaut candidate in 1990, she was joined in NASA Group 13 by three other Stanford graduates—Eileen Collins, Susan Helms, and Jeff Wisoff.

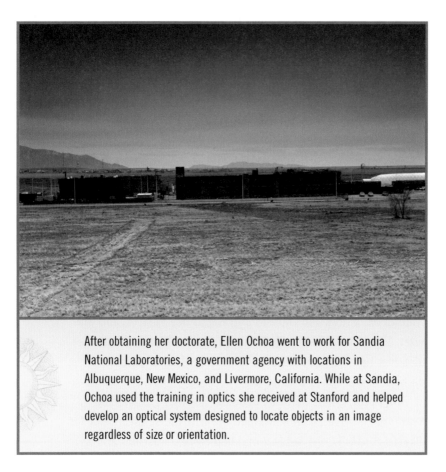

After obtaining her doctorate, Ellen Ochoa went to work for Sandia National Laboratories, a government agency with locations in Albuquerque, New Mexico, and Livermore, California. While at Sandia, Ochoa used the training in optics she received at Stanford and helped develop an optical system designed to locate objects in an image regardless of size or orientation.

Albuquerque, New Mexico, and Livermore, California. Ochoa worked at Sandia's Livermore facility for three years. During her time there, she was able to apply her optical training to help develop an optical system designed to locate objects in an image regardless of size or orientation. She also worked on creating optical methods for different types of image processing, usually conducted by computers.

Optical Work Attracts NASA

Ochoa's work in optical processing was gaining recognition. While she was still at Stanford, Ochoa had worked with Dr. Goodman on an invention they would patent. Goodman applied for a patent entitled "System for enhancement of optical features." Their invention was an optical system that inspects objects. The patent application, dated June 19, 1985, lists professors Goodman and Hesselink and Ellen Ochoa as coinventors. (The patent was assigned on June 23, 1987.) Ochoa applied for two more patents while she was working at Sandia. With coinventors George F. Schils and Donald W. Sweeney, Ochoa applied for a patent called "Position, rotation, and intensity invariant recognizing method," which was an optical object recognition method. With colleagues Jan P. Allebach and Donald W. Sweeney, Ochoa was awarded a third patent, this time for an "Optical ranked-order filtering using threshold decomposition," a method used to remove noise in images. Before reaching her thirtieth birthday, Ochoa already had her name on three patents.

Although she had not yet been selected to be part of an astronaut candidate class, Ochoa was moving closer to achieving that goal. Taking on a new hobby that her brother Monte enjoyed, Ochoa started to take flying lessons. Learning how to fly small aircraft and getting a feel for flight was another skill to put on her already growing résumé. She got her pilot's license in 1988, and accepted a job at NASA's Ames Research Center at Moffett Field Naval Air Station in Mountain View, California. This brought her closer to the NASA inner circle. As one of NASA's research laboratories, Ames "plays a critical role in virtually all NASA missions in support of America's space and aeronautics programs."[33] As chief of the Intelligent Systems Technology Branch, Ochoa supervised a team of 35 fellow engineers and scientists who were working on the research and development of computer systems that could be used for aerospace expeditions.

Ochoa's work was getting noticed not just within her field, but in the Hispanic community as well. In 1989, the Hispanic Engineer National Achievement Awards Corporation (HENAAC) gave Ochoa its Most Promising Engineer or Scientist Award. This award is presented to an individual whose technical accomplishments indicate that he or she will have a promising career in engineering.

Ellen Ochoa, pictured here with fellow Stanford graduate Eileen Collins during the first day of NASA candidate training, was the first Hispanic woman astronaut. Collins and Ochoa were both part of the 23-member Group 13, which reported to Johnson Space Center in Houston, Texas, in July 1990 for training.

NASA Astronaut Candidate

On January 17, 1990, NASA announced the names of the 23 people who had been selected as Group 13 astronaut candidates for space shuttle flights. Among the group were pilots, engineers, and scientists who would serve as space shuttle pilots and mission specialists on future space shuttle missions. The 23 men and women of Group 13 were chosen from 1,945 qualified applicants. Of those, 106 finalists were selected in the fall of 1989, before the final 23 were chosen. Group 13 was nicknamed "the Hairballs" as a reference to their "lucky 13" number. A black cat—another supposedly unlucky symbol— was used in the original emblem patch design. Even though the design was rejected by NASA, the nickname "Hairballs" stuck.

Before reporting to Johnson Space Center in Houston, Texas, for her yearlong training in July 1990, Ochoa had to attend to some very special personal business. While working at the Ames Research Center, Ochoa met and began to date fellow research engineer Coe Fulmer Miles. The couple married on May 27, 1990. Soon after, the newlyweds moved to Houston, where Ochoa would begin her astronaut candidate training.

At Johnson Space Center, Ochoa was part of an elite group of candidates that included Dr. Bernard Andrew Harris, Jr., who would become the first African American to walk in space, and Eileen Collins, who was both the first female space shuttle pilot and the first female shuttle commander.

Ochoa had actually seen a glimpse of what life would be like as a NASA astronaut while she was still working at Sandia. During NASA's 1987 selection round for astronaut candidates, Ochoa spent a week interviewing, going through a medical examination, touring the training facilities, and talking to current astronauts to learn more about the day-to-day aspects of an astronaut's job. Now she and her candidate colleagues would begin the rigorous training program that was designed to test their limits and capabilities.

NASA TRAINING

The training for new astronaut candidates covers a wide range of experiences and learning in a variety of subjects. There are several courses in aircraft safety, including instruction on how to eject, parachute, and survive in the event that an aircraft malfunctions. Both pilot and mission specialists are trained to fly T-38 high-performance jets, which are stationed at Ellington Field Airport near Johnson Space Center in Houston. Flying in these high-speed jets gives the candidates an opportunity to learn to work as part of a team and in an environment where things happen quickly and decisions need to be made under extreme stress.

For their academic training, candidates go through a wide array of science and technical lectures, including orbital mechanics, meteorology, astronomy, and guidance

During astronaut training, pilot and mission specialists fly high-performance jets to become acclimated to the high-stress environment of space flight. Pictured here is Ellen Ochoa during training at Vance Air Force Base in Houston, Texas, in 1993.

and navigation. They obtain a working knowledge of the space shuttle system by attending lectures and studying the information in textbooks and flight operations manuals. In mockups of the flight decks, middecks, and payload bay, candidates experience what it will be like to be inside the shuttle orbiter and learn operations maintenance, and malfunction identification and recovery.

Perhaps one of the most unusual and important experiences for any astronaut candidate is learning how to function in a weightless environment. As part of this training, candidates fly in a modified KC-135 jet and are submerged in the neutral buoyancy tank, or Weightless Environment Training Facility (WETF). While candidates fly aboard the KC-135 (nicknamed the "vomit comet"), the pilot puts the plane into a parabolic trajectory, alternating climbs and descents. During the period of 20 to 30 seconds when the plane is at its highest altitude, weightlessness occurs.

A gentler way to simulate weightlessness is in the water. Wearing pressurized EVA suits, candidates can actually train in a full-scale model of the orbiter payload bay and airlock while they are submerged in a 25-foot (7.6 meter) deep-water tank. Astronauts also have to cope with the extreme acceleration during shuttle liftoff when G-forces reach about 3.2 times the force of gravity that we feel on Earth. All this training is necessary and critical to becoming a successful and qualified astronaut.

Ochoa made it through her training successfully and officially became an astronaut in 1991. She earned the distinction of becoming NASA's first Hispanic female astronaut and part of a growing number of female astronauts at NASA since the first women were accepted into the program in 1978. Back then, Ochoa had tucked away that newspaper article announcing the first six American female astronauts. The shy kid from La Mesa, California, who had worked hard in school and received a good education, no longer had to dream about being an astronaut—she was one.

6

First Hispanic Woman in Space

Ellen Ochoa made it through the first-year astronaut-training program and officially became a member of the NASA astronaut corps in July 1991. Joining the rest of the 19,000 NASA civil service employees and 40,000 contractors to pursue space exploration marked the achievement of one of Ochoa's goals, but it was just the beginning of working toward many other goals to come.

There are many reasons any astronaut candidate would want to be a part of the U.S. space program. NASA has a reputation for being a close-knit "family," where employees work in a nurturing and stimulating environment. The kind of work they do challenges everyone to bring his/her best effort to the job at hand, and everyone works toward an incredibly exciting common goal in a very complex, high-tech field. In an interview, Ochoa explained her view of NASA: "You have this goal out there that's sort of bigger than you and yourself and your own job that everybody is looking toward and is trying to make happen and I think that helps pull people together."[34]

Ellen Ochoa is pictured here in 1993 during parachute training at Vance Air Force Base. Astronauts go through a rigorous training regimen that includes 16 different sets of courses covering all space shuttle–related crew training requirements.

After the first year of training, astronauts continue on with advanced training in preparation for future flight missions. NASA's Mission Operations Directorate's Flight and Systems Branches at the Johnson Space Center are in charge of this advanced training. There are 16 different sets of courses that cover all the space shuttle–related crew training requirements. These range from "guidance, navigation and control systems to payload [anything that a flight vehicle like the space shuttle carries in addition to what is required for its mission during a flight] and deployment and retrieval systems. This advanced training encompasses two specific types of instruction. These are system-related and phase-related training."[35]

PREPARING FOR SPACE FLIGHT

System-related training involves the use of computer-aided instruction in a self-paced, interactive-programmed environment. In this one-on-one training, system instructors control

RODOLFO NERI VELA: NASA'S FIRST HISPANIC ASTRONAUT

NASA currently has eight active astronauts, two candidates in training, and one who retired in 1994 who were born in the United States and are of Hispanic descent. Several other NASA astronauts of Hispanic heritage come from countries around the world, including Costa Rica, Argentina, Brazil, Peru, and Spain. However, it is Mexico that can lay claim to the first Hispanic astronaut in space. Rodolfo Neri Vela, who was born in the Mexican state of Chilpancingo on February 19, 1952, traveled into space as Mexico's first astronaut aboard the space shuttle *Atlantis* on November 26, 1985.

Although he participated in only one space shuttle mission, Neri Vela traveled 2.4 million miles in 108 Earth orbits and logged more than 165 hours in space. Neri Vela also spent time working on the International Space Station for the European Space Agency in Holland from 1989 to 1990 and has written several books, including *Vuelta al Mundo en Noventa Minutos* (*Around the World in Ninety Minutes*). In 1991, Neri Vela was inducted into the International Space Hall of Fame at the New Mexico Museum of Space History.

the simulator software that trainees use in the training sessions and create mock problems that might occur during a real mission, which the trainee must solve. Although system training is designed to provide instruction in orbiter systems, it is not used to train for a specific mission or the cargo included in such a mission. The function of system-related instruction is mainly to familiarize the trainee with what it will feel like to work and live in space. System training must be completed before an astronaut is given a specific mission assignment.

The next stage in training is called phase training. This instruction focuses on the specific skills that an astronaut needs to perform successfully during an actual mission in space. Instruction is conducted in the Shuttle Mission Simulator (SMS), which trains astronauts in all phases of a space mission from liftoff to the return landing. Astronauts continue phase-related training even after they have been assigned to a specific flight mission. This training usually begins about seven months to a year before the astronaut is assigned a shuttle mission launch date.

Like many of her astronaut colleagues, Ochoa spent half her time in training and the other half performing other duties, such as verifying flight software, working as a crew representative for robotics, and working in the Mission Development branch of the Astronaut Office. Ochoa took flights in the KC-135 jet and honed her skills in egress, or exit, training in the pool, an aspect of the astronaut training that several of her colleagues say is their favorite. Mission Specialist Steve Robinson says, "My favorite part is the training for space walking. To do that, you go underwater, you put on a space suit, and they dunk you in the water and you stay down there for about six hours and you simulate what you are doing along a space walk and it is just a fascinating experience to do this. It's challenging, it's hard, and you're very tired when you're done, and it's also a lot of fun."[36] Others consider flight training the best part. Astronaut Joan Higginbotham says, "I think my favorite part of training has been getting to fly on the KC-135 or better known as the 'vomit comet.' It's the only time we get to experience weightlessness on Earth and it was a kick. It was the best thing we ever got to do."[37] Ochoa doesn't talk about training in terms of her most or least favorite part. Instead, she talks about the challenges of being an astronaut:

> One of the biggest challenges of being an astronaut is learning to handle constant bombardment with information. While astronauts have written procedures for virtually everything, sometimes they must make real-time decisions to deviate from the procedures. That's why pre-flight training, done with the luxury of time, is crucial for handling malfunctions during flight. It takes a thorough understanding of the systems and assumptions that go into each step of the procedures to decide when they are appropriate and when they are not.[38]

STS-56 ATLAS-2 DISCOVERY

After two years of rigorous training, Ochoa was assigned to her first shuttle mission—STS-56. She put in another nine months of training for the mission and was about to embark on her first flight. This was a rather quick track for a NASA astronaut. Ochoa said, "I was in training for three years before my first mission, which isn't that long of a wait. Some astronauts have waited 10, even 16 years before they finally go into space!"[39]

Ochoa, the only woman on a five-member crew, trained for the mission with her colleagues—Kenneth D. Cameron, who was named commander of the mission; Stephen S. Oswald, who served as shuttle pilot; and Michael Foale and Kenneth D. Cockrell, who, along with Ochoa, would serve as mission specialists. Cameron, Oswald, and Foale were all veterans of previous shuttle missions, while Ochoa and Cockrell would be making their first flights aboard a space shuttle. Reflecting on her first mission a few years later, Ochoa said:

> [M]y first crew consisted of a Marine test pilot, 2 ex-Navy test pilots, a British laboratory astrophysicist and me—talk about

Ellen Ochoa's first shuttle mission, *STS-56*, was launched on April 8, 1993. Pictured here, from left to right, is the five-member crew: Mission Specialist Kenneth D. Cockrell, Pilot Stephen S. Oswald, Mission Specialist C. Michael Foale, Commander Kenneth D. Cameron, and Mission Specialist Ellen Ochoa.

combining people with vastly different strengths and personalities to reach a common goal! Just designing our mission patch was an interesting collaboration. Our commander wanted it to look as much like the Marine Corps emblem as possible, and especially wanted an eagle on it. My view was that this was an international mission—we were studying an international environmental problem and several of the instruments came from European scientists, so putting such a nationalistic symbol was probably not appropriate. His response was, "Well, it wouldn't have to be an attack eagle, it could be a nurturing eagle!"[40]

The *STS-56* mission was the fifty-fourth NASA shuttle mission, and the sixteenth flight of space shuttle *Discovery*. It was also only the sixth launch to take place at night. The primary focus of the mission was to use the ATLAS-2 (Atmospheric Laboratory for Science and Applications) and Shuttle Backscatter Ultraviolet (SSBUV) to gather information about Earth's climate and environment. Ochoa was just shy of her thirty-fifth birthday when the shuttle *Discovery* launched from the Kennedy Space Center at 1:29 A.M. Eastern Standard Time on Thursday, April 8, 1993. The launch was originally scheduled to take place two days earlier, but an instrument malfunction caused the flight to be postponed. Undaunted by the delay, Ochoa later said:

> When mistakes happen, don't turn them into emergencies. Few failures truly require immediate action. . . . In preparation for a mission, plans are nothing, but planning is everything. When a plan must be scrapped and a new one developed on the fly, the pre-flight work was not done in vain. The ability to develop a new workable plan within hours or days is obviously a result of the months of gathering information, asking questions and understanding all sides of an issue.[41]

WORKING ABOVE THE EARTH

Being a scientist, it was a natural fit for Ochoa to become a mission specialist astronaut. Working with the commander and pilot, the mission specialist has the overall responsibility for the management of the mission operations, including crew activity planning, consumables usage, and experiments and payload operations. On her first mission, Ochoa was busy with the scientific experiments agenda, because the mission's focus was to conduct "atmospheric, climate, and solar studies to determine the effects of solar activity on Earth's environment."[42] The crew studied the amount of ozone loss in Earth's atmosphere, took measurements of various chemicals present in the air, and measured the concentration and amount of energy coming from the sun at different wavelengths to help scientists understand the critical atmospheric chemical reactions that were taking place.

As part of this collection of data process, Ochoa operated the Remote Manipulator System (RMS). This instrument is a 50-foot-long (15-meter-long), six-jointed robotic arm. On April 11, Ochoa used the RMS to deploy the SPARTAN-201, a free-flying scientific instrument platform designed to collect data about the velocity and acceleration of solar wind and to study the sun's corona (outermost atmosphere). Two days later, Ochoa used the RMS to retrieve SPARTAN-201 and return it to *Discovery*'s cargo bay to be carried home.

Free Time on the Mission

Although much of their time was taken up with work, the astronauts did have some free time to enjoy the flight experience. Using the Shuttle Amateur Radio Experiment II (SAREX II), the crew made contact with schools around the world. They also made the first contact with the Russian space station Mir using an amateur radio. As a classical flutist, Ochoa provided music for the crew. She brought along her flute in case she had time to play it in space. For Commander Cameron, a Marine Corps colonel, Ochoa played "The Marine Corps Hymn" before floating over to one of *Discovery*'s windows to peer out at the earth below. Then she began to play selections by composers Vivaldi and Mozart. Using sheet music was easy in the weightless environment. "You can hold the music up and you don't even need a music stand,"[43] Ochoa said with a laugh.

Ochoa and the rest of the crew also e-mailed their families, read, and took in the sights of space from the shuttle's windows. Despite being a scientist at heart, Ochoa's most memorable moments from her first trip into space were not the data collected or the experiments performed. Instead, she was awe-inspired by the sheer beauty of space and the views of Earth so many hundreds of miles away. "I never got tired of watching the Earth, day or night, as we passed over it. Even though we brought back some pretty incredible pictures, they don't quite compare with being there,"[44] said Ochoa.

Living in space, working in a confined area, and not being able to do the usual, everyday things was a new experience. The space environment, particularly the absence of gravity, presents many challenges for astronauts. Tasks as simple as eating, drinking, going to the bathroom, and sleeping become more complicated than normal. Because zero-gravity causes mass muscle loss, astronauts have to spend time in space exercising to help offset this muscle loss. Astronauts typically lose weight in space, so it is important that they eat and that their meals are properly calculated for maximum nutrition.

THE RETURN HOME AND THE NEXT MISSION

The *STS-56 Discovery* mission began with a delay and so did its return. Bad weather delayed the landing of the shuttle at Kennedy Space Center until Saturday, April 17. In the early morning, Commander Ken Cameron safely landed *Discovery* and mission *STS-56* was completed. Counting the time spent in quarantine (isolation)—one week before launch—Ochoa had been away from home for more than two weeks.

Ochoa did not have much time to wonder if she would be assigned to another shuttle mission. She was soon back in training for *STS-66*, a continuation of NASA's Mission To Planet Earth program. This flight, aboard the space shuttle *Atlantis*, would continue NASA's work to collect information about the sun's energy output and the chemical composition of Earth's middle atmosphere to help scientists analyze how these factors affect global ozone levels. It was the third flight of the ATLAS remote-sensing lab. Accompanying the ATLAS was the German-built Shuttle Pallet Satellite (SPAS), which housed two highly sensitive instruments: the Cryogenic Infrared Spectrometers and Telescopes for the Atmosphere (CRISTA) and the Middle Atmosphere High Resolution Spectrograph Investigation (MAHRSI). These instruments would be used to measure the amounts of certain gases and chemicals in the atmosphere and lower thermosphere.

The landing of the *STS-56 Discovery* mission was delayed due to inclement weather, but the space shuttle finally touched down on April 17, 1993, at Cape Canaveral, Florida. Pictured here is *Discovery* on its descent toward the runway.

The *STS-66* mission consisted of six crewmembers. Ochoa would be joined on her second flight by shuttle flight veterans Commander Donald R. McMonagle and Pilot Curtis L. Brown, Jr., along with Scott E. Parazynski, Joseph R. Tanner, and Jean-Francois Clervoy, who would be representing the European Space Agency. Once again, Ochoa found herself the only woman among the crew. On this flight, however, Ochoa was not only a mission specialist; she was also appointed payload commander. This meant she would be in charge of all of *Atlantis*'s scientific studies over the course of the 10-day mission. Because the crew was scheduled to work 24 hours a day, the crewmembers were split up into two teams (red and blue) to work 12-hour shifts each. The red team—McMonagle, Ochoa, and Tanner—worked the first shift, and the blue team of Brown, Clervoy, and Parazynski took the second shift.

ATLANTIS

Atlantis lifted off from Kennedy Space Center at 11:59 A.M. Eastern Standard Time on November 3, 1994. It was a beautiful Thursday morning. Clear skies and pleasant weather provided excellent launch conditions. The only weather concern that morning was a cold front that was approaching the Iberian Peninsula in Europe, where Transatlantic Abort Landing (TAL) sites in Spain and Portugal are located. TAL was created to provide an opportunity for the shuttle to land in an emergency situation such as engine failure or a cabin pressure leak. The flight countdown was temporarily held up, but after 3 minutes and 43 seconds, the go-ahead was given for launch.

Approximately one hour into the flight, the crew was given the "go" for orbit operations. As she had done in her previous mission, Ochoa inspected the robotic arm before putting it into use. Later that afternoon, Ochoa reported that she had successfully grasped the SPAS and was powering up its systems in preparation to deploy it early Friday morning. The crew conducted many atmospheric experiments during the mission. One of Ochoa's responsibilities was to activate the Shuttle Solar Backscatter Ultraviolet (SSBUV) experiment, which was designed to verify atmospheric readings of the ozone and solar ultraviolet light intensity gathered by free-floating NASA satellites. Ochoa was also responsible for retrieving the SPAS satellite and placing it back in the shuttle cargo bay for its return home.

Although there was a lot of work to accomplish, Ochoa had the opportunity to take a brief break to answer questions about her research from high school honor students during an interview on a local Washington, D.C., television station. Ochoa loves science and conducting research, but she also enjoys the educational aspects of her job. She feels that it is very important to get the word out that there are lots of interesting and challenging careers available to people who apply themselves to the study of math and science. Ochoa says, "I've probably given 150 talks over the past few years. I never thought about this aspect of the job when I was applying, but it's extremely rewarding. I'm not trying to make every kid an astronaut, but I want kids to think about a career and the preparation they'll need."[45]

On her second mission, Ochoa took with her the class ring of Stacey Lynn Balascio, a San Diego State University student from Ochoa's hometown, who had been struck by a car and killed just four days before graduation in May 1994. Ochoa was deeply touched by Balascio's death. As a tribute, Ochoa took the ring to a place Balascio would never have the opportunity to go, and then gave the ring to Balascio's parents upon her return from space.

STS-66 was a successful mission, as well as a challenging and rewarding experience for Ochoa. Not even the diverted landing from Florida's Kennedy Space Center to California due to high winds, rain, and cloud cover could dampen the enthusiasm of the crew. *Atlantis* touched down at Edwards Air Force Base on Monday, November 14, at 10:33 A.M.

Ochoa was now a veteran of two NASA space shuttle flights. Being an astronaut fulfilled her both professionally and scholastically. She says, "I always liked school, and being an astronaut allows you to learn continuously, like you do in school. One flight you're working on atmospheric research. The next, it's bone density studies or space station design. . . . What engineer wouldn't want those experiences?"[46]

Ochoa's love of learning had taken her into space twice—two times more than she could have imagined as a young girl watching Neil Armstrong walk on the moon. But would she be assigned to yet another flight into space? That remained to be seen.

7

Destination: International Space Station

Five and a half years passed before Ellen Ochoa made her next shuttle mission. In the meantime, she was far from idle. While she was back on the ground working at Johnson Space Center, Ochoa led the Astronaut Office support to the International Space Station (ISS) program, which was developing flight hardware, as well as training products and procedures. NASA sent 27 shuttles into space between February 1995 and December 1998. In that time, more than 150 astronauts went up in space. A major focus of the missions during this time was the Russian Space Station Mir, which was a first-phase program of the International Space Station. Constructed in orbit over a 10-year period beginning in 1986, Mir (which in Russian means "peace" and "community") gave scientists throughout the world a large laboratory in which they could live while orbiting in space.

The space shuttle–Mir relationship began with the *STS-60* mission in February 1994, when the shuttle *Discovery* launched with

Russian cosmonaut Sergei K. Krikalev on board. The following year, *STS-71*, carrying two Russian cosmonauts, made the first successful docking with the Mir space station. Anatoly Yakovlevich Solovyev and Nikolai Mikhailovich Budarin stayed aboard Mir, while *Discovery* brought home U.S. astronaut Norman E. Thagard, who had flown to the Mir station from Kazakstan in March 1995. *Discovery* also safely returned to Earth cosmonauts Vladimir Nikolaevich Dezhurov and Gennady Mikhailovich Strekalov, who had flown to Mir with Thagard.

The Shuttle-Mir program ended with the *STS-91* mission, in which astronaut Andy Thomas transferred from Mir to *Discovery* after spending 130 days at the space station. Mir's 15-year journey ended on March 23, 2001, when, in a controlled de-orbit, it entered Earth's atmosphere and fell safely into the Pacific Ocean near Nadi, Fiji.

The next phase in living in space would begin with a much larger, more ambitious plan—to build an international space station with an interior the size of a 747 airplane. Ochoa would be a part of this next international joint venture.

HONORS AND MOTHERHOOD

While working for NASA, Ochoa was also acting as a goodwill ambassador for the U.S. space program. She gave lectures and visited schools to talk to students. At a talk she was giving at the Pratt School of Engineering at Duke University in 2004, Ochoa said:

> We're very, very committed to the educational aspects of our job. All the astronauts go out and speak to schools all over the country, even outside the United States. In a lot of cases, we're talking to elementary, middle school and high school students. We're talking to them about the importance of math and science education. You have that entree as an astronaut. You're in a position where students will listen to you. They are interested and excited about the subjects you're talking about.[47]

At the same time, Ochoa was also being recognized for her professional achievements. Aside from the two Space Flight Medals she received from NASA in recognition of her missions in 1993 and 1994, she was also awarded two Space Act Tech Brief Awards in 1992 and the Outstanding Leadership Medal in 1995. Other awards she won included the 1994 Women in Science and Engineering's Engineering Achievement Award, the 1995 Hispanic Heritage Foundation Leadership Award, the 1995 Albert V. Baez Award for Outstanding Technical Contribution to Humanity from the Hispanic Engineer National Achievement Awards Corporation (HENAAC), and the 1993 Congressional Hispanic Caucus Medallion of Excellence Role Model Award. Ochoa was also inducted into the HENAAC Hall of Fame in 1995. Not only was she being recognized for her contributions to science and research within her professional community, but she was also being honored for her tireless service to the Hispanic community as well.

Amid the demands of their careers, Ellen and her husband, Coe, became parents on May 24, 1998. They adopted a baby boy they named Wilson, in the old tradition of Ochoa's family. Juggling the demands of motherhood with her career wasn't easy for Ochoa, but she spent as much time as she could with her son when she wasn't in training. After her first mission after they adopted Wilson, Ochoa was asked whether it is hard to be an astronaut and a mother. Ochoa replied, "I think it's hard being anything and a mother. Both are full-time jobs, and you have to work very hard at both to do a good job. Personally, I find both jobs wonderful. It is hard to be separated from my husband and son when I go on a mission, and I miss them a great deal. But lots of people have to be away from their families because of their jobs."[48]

A TRIP TO THE ISS

Ochoa didn't get to spend much time as a new mom before she had to begin training for her next mission. Along with six crewmates, Ochoa was not just going back into space, but to

Ellen Ochoa and her husband, Coe Fulmer Miles, adopted a baby boy named Wilson in 1998. Ochoa is pictured here with her son shortly after she returned from the *STS-96* mission in June 1999.

the International Space Station (ISS). This large, orbiting laboratory was being funded, constructed, and staffed through the joint efforts of 16 nations, including Russia, Japan, Canada, Brazil, and the United States. NASA had helped develop and coordinate the operation of major components and the technical systems of the ISS. Because of the size of its components, the ISS could not be constructed on Earth and then deployed into space. Instead, the components had to be sent up individually and constructed in space. NASA's space shuttle vehicle cargo bays were used to carry these large components into space.

STS-96 was a milestone mission for NASA, the international agencies involved in the ISS program, and the shuttle crew assigned to the mission. Described as a logistical and resupply mission, flight *STS-96* achieved the first-ever docking between a shuttle and the ISS. The primary goal of the mission was to transfer equipment and supplies from the shuttle to the station. Some of the supplies were for the first crews that would live onboard and operate the station. Items for the crews included clothing, computers, medical supplies, and camera equipment. This mission would also be the first time NASA's Integrated Cargo Carrier (ICC), a flatbed pallet housed in *Discovery*'s payload bay, went on a mission. The design of the apparatus allowed cargo to be mounted on both top and bottom. Loaded on the ICC were two space walkers' cranes and a

BEING HISPANIC

ELLEN OCHOA: A ROLE MODEL FOR CHILDREN

Ellen Ochoa's roles both as an astronaut and the first female Hispanic astronaut are irrevocably linked whenever she visits schools or is interviewed by the media. Her Hispanic roots come from her father's side of the family. His parents were Mexican, but he was born in the United States. Her father, Joe, grew up speaking both Spanish and English, but when he had a family of his own, he chose not to speak Spanish in the house. In a 1999 interview, Ochoa said: "When I was growing up, my father believed as many people did at the time that there was a prejudice against people speaking their native language. It's really too bad, and I'm glad that things have changed in recent years."*

As a child growing up in La Mesa, California, Ochoa may not have placed a huge emphasis on her ethnic roots, but when she became an astronaut, she was always identified as "female" and "Hispanic." However, Ochoa has never felt that being Hispanic put any additional pressure on her, nor does it bother her that people tend to play up her Hispanic heritage when she is asked to give a talk or visit with schoolchildren. She believes that it is done with the best of intentions. During an interview, Ochoa explained:

box that housed 400 pounds (181 kilograms) of space-walking tools and flight equipment for use by the astronauts during assembly of the ISS.

THE PERSONAL ASPECTS OF WORK

Ochoa was particularly connected to the *STS-96* mission, having spent two years working tirelessly to coordinate Astronaut Office support for the ISS even before she was assigned to the mission. When asked how she would feel the first time she

The idea is how can we address some of the problems that we see, and some of those problems are that Hispanics don't graduate from high school at the rates that we'd like to see, they don't go on to college at the rate that you would like to see, they don't enter fields like math and science and technology in anywhere near the rate that they exist in the population. So I think that those are all good goals to see if we can encourage some of that to happen at a rate that's more current and commensurate with our population. To me the question isn't so much how I view my heritage, it's, is it meaningful to other people.**

Being an astronaut provides Ochoa with the opportunity to speak to many people, including children with the same background as her own. She believes it is crucial for kids to have a role model, to see what they can grow up to be, and to know that if they work hard, they can accomplish any goal.

* Available online at *http://teachers.scholastic.com/activities/hispanic/ochoaatscript.htm*
** Interview conducted with Ellen Ochoa by author on February 4, 2005.

floated into the station after being part of the lead-up to the mission, Ochoa said, "I see this flight as a culmination of all that work that I did, and I think I'll feel a very personal attachment to the station. I expect I'll also be thinking about the people I worked with, especially the engineers who support the crew office and all the hard work they did to make this a reality."[49]

The *STS-96* crew reflected the global makeup of the ISS. Besides Commander Kent Rominger, Pilot Rick Husband, and mission specialists Daniel Barry, Tammy Jernigan, and Ochoa representing the United States, Russian cosmonaut Valery Tokarev and Canadian astronaut Julie Payette rounded out the seven-member crew.

The complex mission was a big undertaking. A lot of things could go wrong, but Ochoa knew that taking risks was part of being an astronaut and took that knowledge in stride. For Ochoa, going into space was exciting, not scary. Astronauts train very hard to be prepared to handle any problems that might occur. The riskiest part of any flight, according to Ochoa, is the launch, because this is the phase when problems are most likely to happen, as evidenced by the 1986 *Challenger* disaster. Being an astronaut is a career that always carries some risk, but this does not prevent dedicated astronauts like Ochoa from looking forward to doing their jobs.

HUGE TASKS AHEAD

Discovery lifted off from Kennedy Space Center in the early morning hours of May 27, 1999. This time, Ochoa had to say good-bye to both her husband and her son. To try to ease the pain of separation for one-year-old Wilson, Ochoa made a videotape of the two of them doing different things together. While she was gone, her husband, Coe, was able to play the tape for Wilson every evening so he could still see his mother every day, even though she could not be there in person. During the *STS-96* mission, Ochoa was also able to communicate with her husband via e-mail to make sure everything was going all right at home.

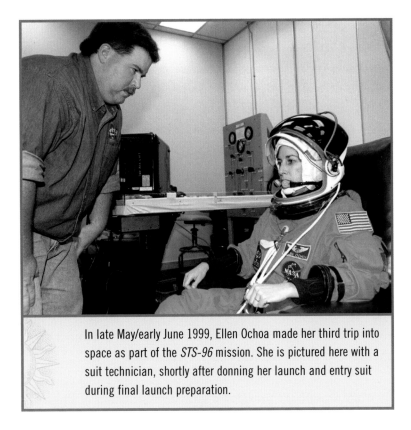

In late May/early June 1999, Ellen Ochoa made her third trip into space as part of the *STS-96* mission. She is pictured here with a suit technician, shortly after donning her launch and entry suit during final launch preparation.

Ochoa had many responsibilities on this mission. During the docking with the ISS, Ochoa operated a program on a laptop computer that plotted the shuttle's trajectory. This information was then communicated to Rominger and Husband as they continued their approach. Once they had docked, Ochoa was responsible for operating the robotic arm. Because the equipment being connected was so large, space walk astronauts Jernigan and Barry actually rode on the robotic arm Ochoa was moving, so that they could hold onto the equipment as the arm moved them into position, where they would place the equipment onto the station. The maneuvers were tricky for Ochoa, because she could not see the arm or the astronauts while she was moving the arm back and forth. Jernigan and Barry's six-hour extravehicular activity (EVA) successfully installed the two crane systems that would be used on future missions to assist with assembly and transfer operations.

To contribute to the educational aspects of space exploration, *Discovery* also brought along a small satellite called Starshine. More than 1,000 schools in the United States and around the globe helped build Starshine. Despite its small size (it was just slightly larger than a basketball), 900 highly polished mirrors covered its exterior, making it visible from the ground. While calculating Starshine's orbit, students had to use several types of mathematics and physics skills.

Having completed a very successful mission, *Discovery* touched down at Kennedy Space Center on the morning of June 6, 1999. As Ochoa had done on her two previous missions, she carried something personal on this one, too. This time, it was something of historic significance—the banner of the National Women's Party. The party had used the banner in the early part of the twentieth century as its members fought to win women one of the most basic rights in a democracy—the right to vote. Five years later, Ochoa said:

> Women's suffrage provided a great representation of diverse views in our political and social system, an important milestone that eventually led to NASA's selection of the first six women astronauts in 1978. Twenty years later, my third mission included three women astronauts as part of the crew, and I was proud to carry that banner in honor of all of the women who had come before us.[50]

ONE LAST FLIGHT INTO SPACE

Many astronauts spend years training and waiting to be assigned to a mission. Senator John Glenn made an unprecedented second flight into space on the *STS-95* mission, 35 years after his first space flight. When Ochoa was named to the *STS-110* crew, it marked her fourth flight into space. In between her 1999 mission and *STS-110*, Ochoa had also had another baby. A son, Jordan, was born to Ochoa and her husband in early April 2000, just 10 months after Ochoa returned from her first trip to the ISS. With two young children at home, Ochoa now had to say

Ellen Ochoa is pictured here with Pilot Stephen Frick in an armored personnel carrier during Terminal Countdown Demonstration Test activities prior to her fourth and final space flight aboard the space shuttle *Atlantis* in April 2002. TCDT training is held prior to each shuttle launch and includes emergency egress training and a simulated launch countdown.

good-bye to them as she prepared for another flight to the ISS.

STS-110 Atlantis was the thirteenth shuttle flight to the ISS. Mission Specialist Jerry Ross was going on his seventh mission, a milestone in human space flight. Joining Ross were Commander Michael Bloomfield, Pilot Stephen Frick, and mission specialists Steven Smith, Lee Morin, Rex Walheim, and Ellen Ochoa. Again, Ochoa found herself the lone female member of the crew.

STS-110 Mission Goals

Atlantis lifted off from Kennedy Space Center at 4:45 P.M. on April 8, 2002. Among the many objectives of this mission was the installation of the S0 truss (S-Zero)—the first of nine pieces that would make up the ISS's external framework. When the nine pieces are all in place, the ISS will measure 356 feet (109 meters) across. Ochoa played a major role in accomplishing this objective, as she lifted the truss out of *Atlantis*'s payload bay with the ISS's robotic arm. After removing it from the cargo bay, Ochoa and station crewmember Dan Bursch maneuvered the truss onto a clamp at the top of the Destiny Lab. It took four space walks to attach the truss to Destiny. The crew also transferred critical supplies to the ISS, including water and technical equipment.

Ochoa was surprised by how much the ISS had grown since her previous flight. She said,

> It was amazing to see how the space station has grown between those two flights, from an uninhabited two-module spaceship into a gleaming 150-ft long laboratory and home to three crewmembers. It also has about 130 feet of truss structure running perpendicular to that, which will eventually hold the large power-producing solar arrays, one of which is in orbit today, brilliant gold gossamer wings that are breathtaking to see as the shuttle approaches and departs the space station.[51]

Whether this would be the last time Ochoa would venture into space, she did not know, but she never tired of the spectacular sights seen through the tiny windows of the shuttle or on the ISS. Ochoa would always be thrilled by the simple beauty of the stars, space, and Earth seen from a vantage point most people can only imagine.

NEW CHALLENGES

In December 2002, Ochoa was appointed deputy director of Flight Crew Operations at the Johnson Space Center. In her new role, Ochoa would be part of the management of the astronaut division. It was not as glamorous as lifting off into space, but the job carried critically important responsibilities. Instead of training for a mission, Ochoa began to oversee the activity of the Astronaut Office and the Aircrafts Ops division.

She handled human resources issues, tracked budget resources, and attended technical and safety meetings. As the deputy in charge, Ochoa also attended debriefings by the flight crews. Of course, Ochoa also continued to visit schools and give talks about NASA and the space program. She always treasured her time with her colleagues:

> You do learn so much from the people that you fly with and train with, and so on a personal level I think that's something I've really gotten out of the astronaut office—learning how to be a member of a team, learning how to lead a team. I went to a lot of the other astronauts for guidance on that and have learned a lot through them. And of course, my best friends now are people in the corps, so on a personal level I think of that as a rewarding experience as well as professional.[52]

8

Return
to Flight

Nothing could have prepared Ellen Ochoa for what happened on her
first mission as deputy director of Flight Crew Operations. When
communications were abruptly cut off between Houston MCC
CAPCOM (Mission Control Center Spacecraft Communicator)
Charlie Hobaugh and *Columbia* Commander Rick Husband during
reentry, all focus turned to every NASA member's worst fear: a
major malfunction in a shuttle mission. As Ochoa moved to assist
with the declaration of the Emergency Contingency Action Plan,
what thoughts ran through her mind? Undoubtedly, her training
guided her to do what needed to be done. She helped the Flight
Crew Operations director (FCOD) make decisions involving the
flight crew and their immediate families, and later, helped assign
FCOD personnel to support the mishap investigation teams.

Had Ochoa ever thought about the dangers of space flight or of
being an astronaut? Certainly she was well aware of the *Challenger*
explosion during liftoff in 1986, even though she wasn't selected as

an astronaut candidate until four years later. Even if Ochoa did not allow herself to think about the catastrophic dangers of her flights, her brother Wilson offered some of his own thoughts on the dangers of Ochoa's job as a space explorer:

> Of course, now I'm much more aware of what could happen. I think I was a little blissfully ignorant. It never ever occurred to me to be worried about the landing. There was always some concern taking off, but we knew that NASA had done so much to prevent what had happened before. . . . On all four of my sister's flights, once she was up and orbiting, the worry factor just wasn't there. I knew she was doing what she wanted to do and having a good time and it never occurred to me that the landing was something to be concerned about. . . . As far as mom being worried about the safety, she was like all of us [kids]. We all have the feeling that what [Ellen] was doing is important, and if you're doing something you love, something you want to do then it's worth whatever risk there is.[53]

A TIME TO MOURN, A TIME TO HONOR

In the immediate aftermath of the disintegration of *Columbia*, NASA personnel began the grim task of locating and collecting the thousands of twisted, contorted fragments of the space shuttle that left a trail across more than 500 square miles (1,295 square kilometers) of eastern Texas and parts of Louisiana. They were under a time constraint, as curious onlookers might disturb a site of debris, or worse, remove pieces of evidence before NASA had a chance to collect it.

One of Ochoa's immediate tasks was to help coordinate the gathering of the remains of the shuttle crew. She was personally touched by the tragedy not only as a member of the NASA organization that had lost seven of its own, but as a crewmate of Rick Husband on mission *STS-96*. Ochoa helped plan memorial services for *Columbia*'s crew and attended most of them personally. Understandably, it was a very difficult time for everyone in the NASA "family."

On February 1, 2003, the space shuttle *Columbia* disintegrated above Texas upon reentry into the earth's atmosphere, killing all seven astronauts on board. Here, a visitor takes a photo of the wreaths displayed at the memorial site in Hemphill, Texas, during the first anniversary of the shuttle disaster.

Memorial services were held for the crew and their families on February 4, 2003, at the Johnson Space Center in Houston, Texas, site of Mission Control. Those in attendance included President George W. Bush and former astronauts John Glenn and Neil Armstrong. Speaking on behalf of NASA, administrator Sean O'Keefe said:

> Throughout our proud NASA family, the bond between those who venture into space—our outstanding astronaut corps—and those who make space flight possible—our dedicated scientists, engineers, safety and support personnel—is incredibly strong. Today, our grief is overwhelming.
>
> Our duty now is to provide comfort to the brave families of the *Columbia* crew—the families who take so much pride in their loved one's remarkable accomplishments.

We also have the tremendous duty to honor the legacy of these seven fallen heroes by finding out what caused the loss of *Columbia* and its crew, to correct what problems we find, and to make sure this never happens again. We owe this to you, the families, and to the American people. With an uncompromising commitment to safety, we will keep this solemn pledge.[54]

A few days later, Vice President Richard (Dick) B. Cheney was joined by O'Keefe at the Washington National Cathedral in Washington, D.C., for a private memorial service to honor the crew of space shuttle *Columbia*. Holding their own memorial on February 7, thousands of workers who had launched *Columbia* on its final flight gathered on what would have been its landing strip at the Kennedy Space Center in Cape Canaveral, Florida.

What Went Wrong?

Besides dealing with the emotional and psychological impact of the tragic loss of their seven colleagues, NASA employees had the tough job of trying to find out what happened that caused *Columbia* to break apart during its reentry into Earth's atmosphere. There was plenty of speculation as to the cause or causes of the accident. Was it a terrorist attack? Had the orbiter been struck by some space debris?

Quietly, many people were wondering if the orbiter had been damaged during liftoff 16 days earlier when a chunk of foam the size of a briefcase had fallen away from *Columbia*'s external fuel tank and hit the orbiter's left wing. At a relative speed of 500 miles per hour (805 kilometers per hour), had the foam strike caused irreparable damage? NASA officials had seen the foam hit the orbiter wing while reviewing video footage of the liftoff, even as *Columbia*'s crew was conducting various experiments in space. After spending several hours reviewing the tape of the launch and analyzing what an accident like the foam strike might do to the spacecraft, NASA personnel on the ground were comfortable in concluding that the incident was not a critical safety issue. During a press conference after *Columbia*'s breakup, Shuttle Program Manager Ron Dittemore said, "From our experience it was determined that the event did not represent a safety concern."[55]

The day after the *Columbia* accident, O'Keefe announced the formation of the Space Shuttle Mishap Interagency Investigation Board. Its mission was to "provide an independent review of the events and activities that led up to the tragic loss of the seven astronauts Saturday on board the Space Shuttle Columbia."[56] After six months of gathering information, interviewing personnel, and reviewing reports from the various teams, the Columbia Accident Investigation Board (CAIB) released the report of its findings on August 26, 2003. The panel determined that the cause of the accident was, in fact, damage done when the chunk of foam struck the orbiter's left wing, making a hole the size of a basketball. During reentry into the earth's atmosphere, the hole in the wing allowed superheated gases to enter the wing structure, resulting in the destruction of the craft. The board also made 29 specific recommendations to NASA to improve the safety of future shuttle flights. These recommendations included:

- Foam from external tank should not break free
- Better preflight inspection routines
- Increase quality of images available of shuttle during ascent and on-flight
- Recertify all shuttle components by the year 2010
- Establish an independent Technical Engineering Authority that is responsible for technical requirements and all waivers to them, and will build a disciplined, systematic approach to identifying, analyzing, and controlling hazards throughout the life cycle of the Shuttle System.[57]

BACK TO THE DRAWING BOARD

For the next two years, NASA personnel worked to correct the flaws in the shuttle's external fuel tank design (which is where

Although there was great anxiety before the launch of *STS-114*, the first space flight after the *Columbia* disaster, NASA personnel were also excited about resuming space travel. Mission specialists Charles Camarda (left) and Andrew Thomas are pictured here in front of the space shuttle before its launch.

the foam broke off) and to upgrade flight hardware, as well as incorporate cameras and visual tracking and inspection equipment to record the launch of the first shuttle as it lifted off after manned space flight resumed.

The orbiter *Discovery* was selected to take the *STS-114* crew on this mission, in what was dubbed "Return to Flight."

Discovery had also been the first orbiter to launch after the *Challenger* accident 19 years earlier.

The crew of *Discovery*, with Eileen Collins as commander (the first woman to command a space shuttle flight), trained in earnest as they awaited word that NASA was ready to send another shuttle into space. Part of the crew's training included learning how to repair damage to the orbiter while in space, something that the *Columbia* crew had not been trained to do. The Return to Flight mission was critical to the International Space Station (ISS) project as well, since the shuttle was the only spacecraft large enough to transport much of the equipment needed to complete construction of the ISS.

As preparations were made for the return to space, Ochoa had been busy assisting FCOD Robert Cabana. She was juggling many responsibilities, from attending technical meetings and status meetings concerning the return of shuttle missions to monitoring information available about the ongoing design modifications of the space shuttle. She also had to make sure that the business of the Flight Crew Operations department continued during the hiatus in mission launches, maintaining adequate numbers of crewmembers with the appropriate skills to support all American human space flight activities. In addition, she served as a representative for NASA in promoting human space flight program development to the public.

HUMAN SPACE FLIGHT RESUMES

In the spring of 2005, NASA officials were confident that all the necessary modifications had been made and the shuttle *Discovery* was ready to return NASA to the business of human space flight. The shuttle was rolled out of the Vehicle Assembly Building (VAB) at noon on April 1, to begin its four-mile (6.4-kilometers) journey to launchpad 39B, where it was set to lift off on May 15. Unfortunately, glitches in some sensors and a concern about ice breaking away during liftoff postponed the launch until July 26. Finally, with its seven crewmembers—Commander Eileen Collins, Pilot James Kelly, and mission specialists Charles Camarda, Wendy Lawrence, Soichi Noguchi, Steve Robinson, and Andy Thomas—strapped into their launch seats, *Discovery* lifted off into a clear blue sky from the Kennedy Space Center at 10:39 A.M. Eastern Daylight Time. *Discovery* was scheduled to spend 12 days in space, taking much-needed supplies to the ISS crew and conducting two space walks to simulate making repairs to the orbiter.

During the mission, there were many technical and management meetings. The decision-making body is called the Mission Management Team, and Ellen Ochoa is an alternate member (the director is the prime member).

Not-So-Perfect Liftoff

For *Discovery*'s flight, Ochoa remained in Houston and headed to the MCC about two to three hours before the scheduled launch time. She manned the console for all technical and management discussions before the countdown to liftoff. Everything looked perfect during the launch, and all systems functioned beautifully. However, the more than 100 new cameras that had been put in place to give engineers several views of *Discovery*'s launch captured images showing some type of debris falling away from the external fuel tank two minutes after what had appeared to be a perfect liftoff. Engineers estimated that a foam chunk, between 24 to 33 inches (61 to 84 centimeters) long and 10 to 14 inches (25 to 36 centimeters) wide, flew off soon after the booster rockets dropped away from the spacecraft.

Once *Discovery* was in orbit and on its way to the ISS, NASA officials told the crew what they had seen. That Wednesday, the two-man crew aboard the ISS used cameras to take photos and inspect the spacecraft for any damage to *Discovery*. Fortunately, there was no visible major damage to the orbiter's wing. Later in the mission, astronauts Stephen Robinson and Soichi Noguchi took three space walks, allowing them an up-close look at *Discovery*. On one walk, the two repaired a broken gyroscope on the ISS. On another day, they went outside to test new shuttle repair materials and

A SCHOOL NAMED IN HER HONOR

Most people aren't lucky enough to earn recognition for their accomplishments while they are still alive, but Ellen Ochoa's legacy as the first Hispanic woman in space has led one Washington State community to name a school after her. Located at the confluence of the Columbia, Yakima, and Snake rivers in the southeast corner of the state lies the city of Pasco. Although the population of Pasco is diverse, more than half of its residents are Hispanic and the Hispanic population is growing. Most are descendants of migrant families that originally settled in the area. In 2001, the city approved construction of a middle school to better serve the needs of its growing Hispanic population. Construction on the district's 109,000-square-foot (10,126-square-meter) school began in January 2001 and was completed and ready for the 2002–2003 school year.

The members of the local school board wanted to name their new school after someone with a Hispanic heritage. They selected Ellen Ochoa. Although Ochoa had never visited Pasco, Washington, before, she was invited to participate in the school's dedication ceremonies. She said, "I got to be there at the dedication of the school . . . and what bigger honor could you have to think that people thought enough of your impact on students, that they would name a school after you. People at that school will learn at least a little something about my background that maybe will make them think about their own lives and their own futures."*

Ochoa told the middle-school students of the new school what she had said to so many other students at schools across the country—that they could achieve success as she had done, through hard work and dedication. Ochoa's visit showed the students of Ellen Ochoa Middle School that all things are possible and gave them a tangible goal. For Ellen Ochoa, what better lasting legacy could there be?

* Interview conducted with Ellen Ochoa by author on February 4, 2005.

Ellen Ochoa serves as an excellent role model, both for young women and for Hispanic Americans, as she speaks out about issues that are important to her. Pictured here, left to right, are Ochoa, Joan Higginbotham, Yvonne Cagle, and former astronaut Sally Ride at a panel discussion at the Kennedy Space Center in Cape Canaveral, Florida.

techniques in the event that they might be necessary on future shuttle flights.

The most dangerous of the space walks came on Wednesday, August 2. NASA officials on the ground noticed that two pieces of filler material were dangling from the orbiter's underbelly. Concerned that the fabric could cause problems for *Discovery* during its reentry, NASA decided that an attempt should be made to remove the material. Robinson would be maneuvering underneath *Discovery*—a feat never tried before—on the end of the ISS's 58-foot (17.7-meters) robot arm. Once within reach, Robinson would try to remove the dangling filler without damaging the orbiter. Robinson managed to tug on the strips with his gloved hands, pulling the material away.

The Start of a New Era

Nothing about *STS-114*'s mission was routine. Even the weather interfered with *Discovery*'s scheduled landing. Instead of returning home on Monday, August 8, *Discovery* had to circle the earth for an additional day because of scattered showers and lightning storms. Then, on Tuesday, August 9, the weather was still not good over Kennedy Space Center in Florida, so *Discovery* was diverted to Edwards Air Force Base in California. Finally, after being away for 14 days, circling the earth 219 times, and traveling 5.8 million miles (9.3 million kilometers) in space, *Discovery* touched down safely at 8:11 A.M. Although the *Discovery* mission, Ochoa's second shuttle mission as deputy director of FCOD, was a success in many ways, there have only been two missions since (in July and September of 2006). While the space shuttle program gets back on its feet, Ochoa will continue to visit schools and talk to children about space exploration as a career.

What better role model for the astronauts of the future than Ellen Ochoa? Just as her mother, Rosanne, who passed away on April 9, 2005, always emphasized the importance of education, Ochoa, too, is working hard to instill in the next generation of space explorers the importance of education and the belief that people can accomplish anything through hard work and dedication, regardless of race, ethnicity, or gender.

Chronology and Timeline

1957   Soviet space satellite *Sputnik 1* orbits Earth.

1958   National Aeronautics and Space Agency (NASA) created; Lauri Ellen Ochoa born on May 10 in Los Angeles, California.

1959   The Ochoa family moves to La Mesa, California, where Ellen's father is promoted to superintendent of the San Diego Sears store.

1961   American astronaut Alan B. Shepard, Jr., completes 15-minute suborbital flight aboard *Freedom 7*.

1969   *Apollo* 11 astronaut Neil Armstrong is first human to walk on the moon; Ellen Ochoa graduates from Northmont Elementary School.

1971   Begins to attend Grossmont High School.

1972   Parents Joe and Rosanne divorce; Ellen and her siblings remain with Rosanne.

1975   Graduates as valedictorian of her class at Grossmont High School; begins freshman year at San Diego State University.

1978   First six women are selected to the NASA astronaut corps.

1980   Earns Bachelor of Science degree in physics and is again valedictorian of her graduating class; begins postgraduate work at Stanford University.

1981   Earns master's degree from Stanford University.

1983   Sally Ride becomes first American woman in space aboard shuttle *Challenger STS-7*.

1985   Awarded Ph.D. in electrical engineering from Stanford University; joins Imaging Technology Branch of Sandia National Laboratories in Livermore, California, as a research engineer; first applies to NASA's astronauts program and makes it to the top 100 finalists in 1987.

1988 Joins NASA's Ames Research Center in Mountain View, California; receives her private pilot's license.

1990 Becomes one of 23 candidates selected by NASA for the astronaut program; becomes the twenty-second female astronaut and first female Hispanic-American NASA astronaut; marries Coe Fulmer Miles on May 27; moves to Houston to begin astronaut training.

1993 Makes first space flight aboard the shuttle *Discovery* (*STS-56*).

1994 Makes second flight into space aboard the shuttle *Atlantis*.

1998 Son Wilson Miles-Ochoa is adopted in May.

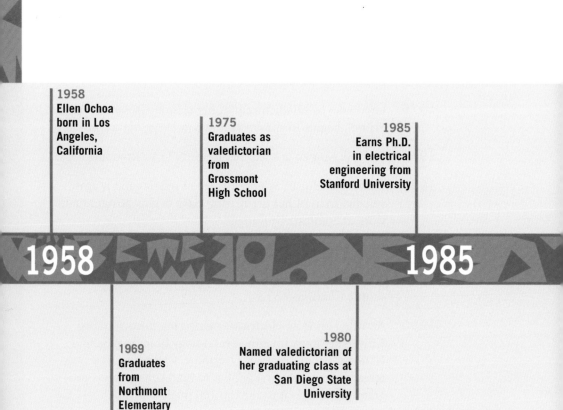

1958
Ellen Ochoa born in Los Angeles, California

1975
Graduates as valedictorian from Grossmont High School

1985
Earns Ph.D. in electrical engineering from Stanford University

1958 1985

1969
Graduates from Northmont Elementary School

1980
Named valedictorian of her graduating class at San Diego State University

1999	Makes third flight into space aboard shuttle *Discovery*.
2000	Son Jordan Miles-Ochoa is born in April.
2002	Makes fourth flight into space aboard shuttle *Atlantis*; appointed deputy director of Flight Crew Operations at the Johnson Space Center.
2003	Is at Mission Control at Johnson Space Center when space shuttle *Columbia* breaks up over Texas during its return from space on February 1, 2003.
2005	Mother, Rosanne Ochoa, dies on April 9; NASA resumes space flights with *STS-114* Return to Flight mission.

1990
Becomes twenty-second female astronaut and first female Hispanic-American NASA astronaut

1999
Makes third flight into space aboard shuttle *Discovery*

2005
NASA resumes space flights

1990

2005

1993
Makes first flight into space aboard the shuttle *Discovery*

2003
Appointed deputy director of Flight Crew Operations at the Johnson Space Center

Notes

Chapter 1

1 Research Mission, FREESTAR. Columbia OV-102, Memo.pdf. *STS-107 Overview, Space Research and You*. Available online at *http://www-pao.ksc.nasa.gov/kscpao/shuttle/summaries/pdf/sts107memo.pdf.*

2 Nancy Gibbs, "Seven Astronauts, One Fate," *Time*, February 10, 2003, 33.

3 Jeffrey Kluger, "What Went Wrong?" *Time*, February 10, 2003, 39.

4 Interview conducted with Ellen Ochoa by author on February 4, 2005.

5 The Space Shuttle Launch Team. Available online at *http://science.ksc.nasa.gov/shuttle/countdown/launch-team.html.*

6 Jeffrey Kluger, "What Went Wrong?" 41–42.

7 Ibid., 39.

8 Excerpt from Flight Crew Operation Director Contingency Action Plan, e-mailed by Elaine B. Kemp CPS, Secretary to the Director, Flight Crew Operations, NASA.

Chapter 2

9 Ian Ridpath, *Star Tales: Chapter One, Stars and Storytellers*. Available online at *http://www.ianridpath.com/startales/startales1a.htm*

10 Tom D. Crouch, *The National Aeronautics and Space Administration* (New York: Chelsea House Publishers, 1990, 15).

11 Ibid., 33.

12 X-1 TIMELINE. Available online at *http://www.chuckyeager.org/htm_docs/x1tmln.shtml.*

13 William F. Mellberg, *Moon Missions: Mankind's First Voyages to Another World* (Vergemes, Vt.: Plymouth Press, Ltd., 1997), 25.

14 Ibid., 33.

15 NASA's Origins And The Dawn of The Space Age: Monographs in Aerospace History #10, Forward, Roger D. Launius Chief Historian National Aeronautics and Space Administration July 1, 1998. Available online at *http://www.hq.nasa.gov/office/pao/History/monograph10/*

Chapter 3

16 Interview conducted with Ellen Ochoa by author on February 4, 2005.

17 Jack Williams, "Rosanne Ochoa, 84; Graduated from SDSU 22 years after start," *San Diego Union Tribune*, April 15, 2005.

18 Barbara Marvis, *Famous People of Hispanic Heritage, Volume I* (Childs, Md.: Mitchell Lane Publishers, 1996), 84.

19 Interview conducted with Ellen Ochoa by author on February 4, 2005.

20 Interview conducted with Wilson Ochoa by author on July 11, 2005.

21 Ibid.

22 Ibid.

Chapter 4

23 Ibid.

24 Ibid.

25 Barbara Marvis, *Famous People of Hispanic Heritage*, 84–85.

26 Interview conducted with Ellen Ochoa by author on February 4, 2005.

27 Anne Hart, *Without Limits*. Available online at

http://www.graduatingengineer.
com/articles/minority/11-12-
99.html

28 Jeanette Rankin Foundation
Annual Awards Dinner,
June 24, 2004. Available online
at *http://www.rankinfoundation.*
org/events/Dr.Ochoasspeech.htm

Chapter 5

29 Interviews conducted by the
author via e-mail with
Dr. Joseph W. Goodman,
February 22 and 25, 2005.

30 Ibid.

31 Impacto, Influencia, Cambio.
Science, Technology, and
Invention in Latin America and
the Southwestern United States,
Smithsonian Office of
Education: Dr. Ochoa's
Biographical Sketch. Available
online at *http://www.smithsoni-*
aneducation.org/scitech/impacto/
graphic/ellen/biography.html

32 Jeanette Rankin Foundation
Annual Awards Dinner,
June 24, 2004. Available online at
http://www.rankinfoundation.
org/events/Dr.Ochoasspeech.htm

33 About NASA Ames
Research Center. Available
online at *http://www.nasa.gov/*
centers/ames/about/aboutames-
centerOverview.html

Chapter 6

34 Ibid.

35 Lift-Off to Space Exploration:
Human Journey, Selection and
Training of Astronauts. Available
online at
http://liftoff.msfc.nasa.gov/
academy/astronauts/training.html

36 Astronaut Flight Lounge.
Astronaut Steve Robinson. "Ask
an Astronaut a Question."
Available online at
http://www.nasa.gov/exter-
nalflash/afl/index_noaccess.htm

37 Ibid.

38 Dawn Levy, "Stay Cool Under
Pressure, Astronaut Ellen Ochoa
Tells Phi Beta Kappa Inductees."
Available online at *http://news-*
service.stanford.edu/news/2002/
june19/kappa2002-619.htm

39 "Celebrate Hispanic Heritage:
Meet Famous Latinos-Ellen
Ochoa." *Teacher Scholastic.*
Available online at
http://teacher.scholastic.com/
activities/hispanic/
ochoatscript.htm

40 Anne Hart, *Without Limits.*
Available online at
http://www.graduatingengineer.
com/articles/minority/11-12-
99.html

41 Dawn Levy, "Stay Cool Under.
Pressure, Astronaut Ellen Ochoa
Tells Phi Beta Kappa Inductees."

42 Anne Hart, *Without Limits.*

43 Miles O'Brien, "Getting to Know
the Crew of STS-96." *CNN*
Interactive. Available online at
http://www.cnn.com/TECH/
space/9905/24/downlinks/
index.html.

44 Hispanic Heritage: Ellen
Ochoa. Biography Resource
Center, The Gale Group.
Available online at
*http://www.galegroup.com/free_*
resources/chh/bio/ochoa_e.htm#

45 Stanford University School of
Engineering Annual Report
1997–98. Ellen Ochoa, PhD, '85,
MS, '81. Electrical Engineering:
A Higher Education. Available
online at

http://soe.stanford.edu/AR97-
98/ochoa.html
46 Ibid.

Chapter 7

47 Pratt School of Engineering,
Duke University. *Veteran
Astronaut Boosts Human
Spaceflight in Pratt Appearance.*
Available online at
*http://www.pratt.duke.edu/news/
releases/index.php?story=142.*
48 "Celebrate Hispanic Heritage:
Meet Famous Latinos-Ellen
Ochoa." *Teacher Scholastic.*
Available online at
*http://teacher.scholastic.com/activ
ities/hispanic/ochoatscript.htm*
49 La Prensa San Diego. *Discovery
Begins Mission to International
Space Station,* Volume XXIII
Number 21 ~ May 28, 1999. Preflight interview: Ellen Ochoa
(provided by NASA). Available
online at *http://laprensa-
sandiego.org/archieve/may28/
ochoa.htm*
50 Jeanette Rankin Foundation
Annual Awards Dinner, June 24,
2004. Available online at
*http://www.rankinfoundation.org
/events/Dr.Ochoasspeech.htm*

51 Ibid.
52 Interview conducted with Ellen
Ochoa by author on February 4,
2005.

Chapter 8

53 Interview conducted with
Wilson Ochoa by author on
July 11, 2005.
54 Remarks by the Honorable Sean
O'Keefe, NASA Administrator,
STS-107 Crew Memorial
Ceremony. Available online at
*http://www.spaceref.com:16080/
news/viewpr.html?pid
=10661.*
55 Jeffrey Kluger, "What Went
Wrong?" *Time,* February 10,
2003, 42.
56 NASA Announces Space Shuttle
Columbia Accident Investigation
Board (The Gehman Board).
Available online at
http://www.spaceref.com:16080/
news/viewpr.html?pid=10624.
57 Columbia Accident Investigation
Board. Available online at
*http://en.wikipedia.org/wiki/Colu
mbia_Accident_Investigation_
Board.*

Bibliography

Crouch, Tom D. *The National Aeronautics and Space Administration*. New York: Chelsea House Publishers, 1990.

Gibbs, Nancy. "Seven Astronauts, One Fate." *Time*, February 10, 2003.

Hart, Anne. *Without Limits*. Available online at *http://www.graduatingengineer.com/articles/minority/11-12-99.html*

Jeanette Rankin Foundation Annual Awards Dinner, June 24, 2004. Available online at *http://www.rankinfoundation.org/events/Dr.Ochoasspeech.htm*.

Kluger, Jeffrey. "What Went Wrong?" *Time*, February 10, 2003.

Marvis, Barbara. *Famous People of Hispanic Heritage, Volume I*. Childs, Md.: Mitchell Lane Publishers, 1996, 84.

Mellberg, William F. *Moon Missions: Mankind's First Voyages to Another World*. Vergemes, Vt.: Plymouth Toy & Book, 1997.

Paige, Joy. *Ellen Ochoa: First Hispanic Woman In Space*. New York: The Rosen Publishing Group, Inc., 2004.

Further Reading

Iverson, Teresa. *Ellen Ochoa: Hispanic-American Biographies.* Chicago: Heinemann-Raintree, 2005.

Laezman, Rick. *100 Hispanic-Americans Who Shaped American History.* San Mateo, Calif.: Bluewood Books, 2003.

Lobb, Nancy. *16 Extraordinary Hispanic-Americans.* Portland, Maine: Walch, 1995.

Marsh, Carole. *Ellen Ochoa: First Hispanic-American Woman in Space.* Peachtree, Ga.: Gallopade International, 2003.

Palmisano, Joseph M. *Notable Hispanic-American Women, Book II.* Farmington Hills, Mich.: Thomas Gale Publishing, 1998.

Romero, Maritza. *Great Hispanics of Our Time: Ellen Ochoa.* New York: Powerkids Press, 1998.

St. John, Jetty. *Hispanic Scientists.* Mankato, Minn.: Capstone Press, 1996.

Walker, Pam. *Meet Ellen Ochoa.* Danbury, Conn.: Children's Press, 2000.

Web Sites

NASA Group 8
http://www.astronautix.com/astrogrp/nas81978.htm

NASA Group 13
http://www.astronautix.com/astrogrp/nas31990.htm

Discover Space Station
http://www.discovery.com/stories/science/iss/iss.html

History of NASA
http://www.hq.nasa.gov/office/pao/History/40thmerc7/intro.htm

NASA—Mercury Program
http://www.mercury13.com/

Return to Flight: Space Shuttle Discovery
http://www.msnbc.msn.com/id/8740388/

NASA's First 100 Human Space Flights
http://www.nasa.gov/centers/kennedy/news/facts/hundred-toc.html

Ellen Ochoa Middle School
http://www.scm-ae.com/schools/ochoa.htm

Ellen Ochoa Biography
*http://www.smithsonianeducation.org/scitech/impacto/graphic/ellen/
biography.html*

Shuttle-Mir History
http://spaceflight.nasa.gov/history/shuttle-mir/index.html

First Women in Space
http://www.spacetoday.org/History/ManInSpaceFirsts/FirstGals.html

International Space Station Launches
http://www.spacetoday.org/SpcStns/ISSschedule99.html

Index

Picture Credits

About the Author

Judy L. Hasday, a native of Pennsylvania, received her B.A. in communications and her M.Ed. in instructional technologies from Temple University. She has written many books for young adults, including New York Public Library "Books for the Teen Age" award winners *James Earl Jones* (1999) and *The Holocaust* (2003), and *Extraordinary Women Athletes,* a National Social Studies Council "2001 Notable Social Studies Trade Book for Young People."